THE HORIZONTAL JUMPS

THE HORIZONTAL JUMPS

Planning for Long Term Development

By

NICK NEWMAN, M.S.

JumPR Publishing
2012

Copyright ©2012 by Nick Newman
All rights reserved

ISBN-13: 978-1467979009
ISBN-10: 1467979007

Library of Congress Control Number: 2012910039

Printed in the United States of America

JumPR Publishing
Long Beach, California

www.jumPRathletics.com
Contact: Nick@jumPRathletics.com

Contents

Preface	1
Preface	3
Special Thanks	5
About the Author	7
Chapter 1 - Introduction	9
Introduction	11
About the Long Jump	13
About the Triple Jump	14
History of the Events	14
Horizontal Jumps of Today	15
Looking to the Future	16
Major Marks in the Horizontal Jumps	18
Chapter 2 - Technical Components of the Horizontal Jumps	19
The Long Jump	21
The Approach Run	21
The Takeoff	23
The Flight	26
The Landing	26
Long Jump Picture Guide	28
The Triple Jump	30
The Initial Takeoff and Hop Phase	30
The Step Phase	32
Exercise Drills	35
Common Technical Faults & Causes	36
Chapter 3 - Needs Assessment of the Horizontal Jumps	37
Speed	42
Strength	44
Specific Strength	45
Maximal Power	47
Rate of Force Development	47
Reactive Power	48
General Fitness Components	48
Flexibility	48

Coordination	49
Work Capacity/Endurance	49
Specific Testing Protocols and Standards	49
Test Description	50
Male Testing Standards	53
Female Testing Standards	54

Chapter 4 - Training Principles Applied to the Horizontal Jumps — 55

Acceleration Development	57
Maximum Velocity Development	59
Speed Endurance Development	61
Components of Strength Development	62
General Strength	62
Maximum Strength	63
Maximal Load Method	64
Maximal Eccentric Load Method	65
Maximal Isometric Method	66
Power Development	67
Speed Repetition Method	67
Contrast Loading Method	68
Plyometric Training	70
Rest/Recovery	72
Overreaching	72
Overtraining	73
Preventing Overtraining	74
Common Recovery Methods	74
Passive Recovery	74
Active Recovery	75
Cryotherapy	75
Thermotherapy	75
Massage	75

Chapter 5 – Periodization of Individual Training Components — 77

Warm-up/Cool Down	80
Guidelines for Sprint/Jumps Specific Warm-up	81
Speed Development	81
Strength & Power Development	82
Prime Weight Room Exercises and Polymentric Exercises	86
Technical Development	87
General Fitness Development	90
Concepts of the Periodized Strength Training Program	91

Flexible Undulating Weight Training Program (American Influence)	91
Linear Weight Training Program (European Influence)	96

Chapter 6 - The Periodized Training Programs — 97

Concepts of the Periodized Training Program	99
Training Load Distribution	102
The Weekly Plan	104
American Influenced Weekly Plan	104
European Influenced Weekly Plan	105
Individual Training Phases	106
General Preparation Phase	107
Weekly Loading Chart – USA	109
Weekly Loading Chart – European	109
Special Physical Conditioning	110
Special/Technical Preparation	112
Daily Loading Chart – Specific Physical Conditioning	114
Daily Loading Chart – USA	114
Daily Loading Chart – European	115
Competition Phase	115
Combining the Training Phases	119
Single Periodized Season	119
Double Periodized Season	120
Loading Chart for Full Season	121
Tapering/Peaking	122
Considerations for a Taper	122
Training Intensity	122
Training Volume	122
Duration of the Taper	123
Periodized Model for Taper	123
Tapering Guidelines	124

Chapter 7 - Sample Training Programs — 125

USA Influence System	127
4 Week General Preparation – USA Influence Non-Linear	129
3 Week Specific Physical Conditioning – USA Influence Non-Linear	133
3 Week Technical Training – USA Influence Non-Linear	136
3 Week SPC – USA Influence Option B	139
3 Week Technical Training – USA Influence Option B	142
Example of Early Season Competition Week – USA Influence	145
Example of Main Season Competition Week – USA Influence	146
Example of Peak Season Competition Week – USA Influence	147

   European Influenced Program   148
   4 Week General Preparation – European Influence   149
   3 Week Specific Physical Conditioning – European Influence   153
   3 Week Special/Technical Preparation – European Influence   156
   Example of Early Season Competition Week – European Influence   159
   Example of Main Season Competition Week – European Influence   160
   Example of Peak Competition Week – European Influence   161
   Alternate Set-ups   162

Chapter 8 - Special Exercises Pictures and Descriptions   163
   Plyometric Exercises   165
   Beginner & Intermediate Plyometric Exercises   165
   Advanced Plyometric Exercises   169
   Special Weight Training Exercises   172
   Medicine Ball Exercises   179
   Training Inventory Exercise Descriptions   180
   Jumping Events – Exercise Inventory   193

Final Thoughts   195
   101 General Tips for the Horizontal Jumps   198

PREFACE

Introduction to the purpose of book and information about the author

Nick Newman
The Horizontal Jump: Planning for Long Term Development

Preface

The horizontal jumps are one of the oldest athletic disciplines in the world. They have more than likely existed for thousands of years in one form or another. Although its longevity as a sport has never been in question, from a developmental standpoint, many questions have arisen. For example, why has the long jump been at a near standstill since 1968?

Performance in the majority of track and field events has developed significantly over the last 40 years, with the exception of the long jump. The long jump world record has increased only 5 cm over that time span. The triple jump is also an event which has been stagnant since the days of Jonathan Edwards. Is this a result of poor training? Have coaches today overcomplicated training methods? Has talent selection for track and field suffered with the emergence of more lucrative high profile sports?

The need for investigation is obvious. Over the last decade, more scientific analyses specific to these two events have been produced than ever before. Training scrutiny, however, is still lacking throughout the literature across a broad spectrum and needs to be addressed in order to advance the sport.

I have spent the best part of the last 5 years researching and writing this book. My research has taken on many forms. It started 5 years before the idea of writing a book even came about. This was when my own personal long jump quest began. I soon began building a library of books, DVDs, published research, unpublished research, and the observation of some great coaches. This time was invaluable as it gave me a great understanding of the sport and the training methods which the athletes follow. I experienced many types of training programs before I settled on the systems described within this book.

The trial and error process I experienced as an athlete before this point was essential for my development as both an athlete and a coach. Before starting this book I had completed 8 years of study within the field of Exercise Science and sport performance.

The final 4 years of study were dedicated specifically to the development of sprinters and jumpers. I spent hundreds of hours emailing, calling and observing coaches from all over the world in order to create a training system which would work for me and my athletes.

As an athlete I was closing in on the magic 8 meter barrier and had seen great progress under my own training systems. I had also begun actively coaching a number of successful jumpers which gave me another valuable perspective on jumps development.

The system which I have developed is an integration of various training systems and experiences from many coaches, countries and eras of horizontal jumpers. I have taken successful aspects of many programs and have learned to balance and intertwine them and have created a system which allows the holistic development of all essential abilities.

Therefore the purpose of this book is to begin tying together successful and proven training methods for elite jumpers which are founded on scientific and coaching literature.

Over the last 50 years there has been limited research published regarding specific training systems for the horizontal jumps. Much of the published literature has included coaches' perspectives on training without scientific evidence as the basis of their rationale. Although it is valuable to know what successful and unsuccessful coaches have practiced, it is important to eliminate trial and error as much as possible. Therefore the need for scientifically proven training systems is vital to the future success of the event.

This book is mainly but not solely intended for track and field coaches and athletes. Although the training program is specifically designed for horizontal jumpers, many of the principles discussed cross over to a variety of speed and power sports.

The systematic approach to long term development portrayed in this book is intended as a valuable tool for coaches, athletes and strength training practitioners in a variety of sports. My intent is to convey this information in a way that is simple and direct, containing applicable methodology and reasoning for all coaches and athletes to use.

Application of these training methods needs to be relevant, individual and long lasting so the athlete can understand and feel what he or she is doing rather than just following instructions in a robotic fashion. At the very least, this book will supply you with the knowledge of what is needed to be a great horizontal jumper.

SPECIAL THANKS

I have many people I would like to thank for their help gathering information and experience for this book. Over the past few years, many very knowledgeable and talented sports performance experts and track and field coaches have given me their insight on many topics covered in this text. For that I am extremely grateful and your time and effort should never go without acknowledgment.

The person who has perhaps taught me the most is Dr. Mike Young. I worked closely with Mike for 3 years and cannot explain how much I have learned from him. Thank you, Mike, for all your time and hard work.

There are many other coaches and sports scientists I would like to thank. Nelio Moura of Brazil and Gary Bourne of Australia are two of the world's top horizontal jumps coaches and have graciously responded to many of my emails although we have never actually met in person. Thank you for your time. I would like to thank John Crotty of UK Athletics for his input into various training topics discussed. John is one of the top jumps coaches to come out of Great Britain and worked closely with me for one year.

To every author of every book and research article I have read I also would like to thank you. Tudor Bompa, Donald. Chu, Mel Siff, Michael Boyle, Vladimir Zatsiorsky, Phillip Graham Smith, Ed Jacoby, Bruce Longden and the list could go on and on.

I would like to thank Dr. William Beam of California State University, Fullerton. Dr. Beam has been a mentor to me throughout my graduate education. Thank you for your patience and understanding; I appreciate you all more than you know.

A special thanks also goes to Greg Gubi who helped format and edit the book. Thank you for your excellent work and patience. Thank you to Day Starns who created the superb front/back cover of the book.

Photographer Tony Duffy, who graciously donated his time for many of the pictures, I thank you so much. Tony is one the very best horizontal jumps photographers in world and is famously known for "the Bob Beamon photograph" which I am sure many have seen. Kirby Lee and my good friend

Ryan Kirkpatrick also contributed pictures for the book and I thank you as well. I would also like to thank American triple jumper Blessing Ufodiama for allowing pictures of her to be used for the book. The historical photos are courtesy of The Lost Century of Sports Collection.

I would also like to extend my thanks to a few people who have helped me throughout my own personal long jump journey. Firstly to Jeremy Croy. Without Jeremy taking a chance and giving me a Track and Field scholarship to attend Tiffin University in Ohio, I would have surely returned to England and continued to play basketball. Jeremy was the only coach who offered me a scholarship. Thank you so much for seeing something in me.

My journey continued to Manhattan College in New York and for this I must thank Dan Mecca. I realize now that Dan was an outstanding coach and I thank you for all you taught me. I also want to thank physical therapists Holly Findlay and Cesar Fajardo and massage therapist Crystal Cosby. All have worked with me extensively and are outstanding at what they do. Without their help there is no way I could continue developing as an athlete.

Finally I want to thank all of my family and friends who have supported me throughout this journey and who never lost faith when things became difficult. Thank you for understanding why this means so much to me and why I have sacrificed so much for my passion. It will all be worth it in the end. Thanks again.

ABOUT THE AUTHOR

I am writing this book following 10 years of studying exercise science with specific emphasis on jumping development. In 2001, I graduated with a two year A-level in Sport Science from Durham Community College in England. I decided to take my studies to America in 2001, where I received my bachelor's degree in Exercise Science from Manhattan College in New York. In 2009, I concluded my education with a master's degree in Human Performance and Sport Psychology from California State University Fullerton.

My initial quest to discover the best ways to improve jumping ability began because I wanted to dunk a basketball. It was my goal to play college basketball in the USA and to jump like the players I watched on TV. I started researching and testing my own jumping programs on myself. I improved my vertical jump from 26 inches to 42 inches over a 3-year period. As my interest in jumping increased, I decided to take on a new challenge and pursue the long jump. This challenge proved to be far more difficult than increasing vertical jump height.

I was and still am amazed at the complexity of this seemingly simple athletic discipline. I reached a high level in 2010 and jumped the 4th longest outdoor distance in Great Britain at 7.77m.

Early in 2012 I opened the season with a new personal best of 7.80m. By then I had been serious about long jumping for several years and was researching the training methods of the best long jumpers in the world. I have been blessed to have communicated with some very accomplished coaches who have been kind enough to answer my questions and give me some of their time.

With the lack of specific information regarding the training of horizontal jumpers, I felt it would be beneficial for athletes and coaches if I were to write a book based on everything I have learned over the past decade. Information written in this book has worked for many jumpers, both past and present. I realize there is more than one way to develop a horizontal jumper and that it would be impossible to create the perfect program.

It was my aim, however, to provide athletes and coaches with a detailed but easy to understand book on the sport that I love. I have spent thousands of hours reading, listening, studying, observing and performing training methods related to the horizontal jumps. I have researched, analyzed and contrasted endless amounts of existing research and coaching literature. I have been very lucky along the way to have learned from some of the best jump coaches in the world and much of their input has formed my methodology today.

Scientifically proven training methods are the staple of what I have gathered and deemed to be the optimal way to train for horizontal jumpers. However, it would be irresponsible of me to ignore certain training methods which have been commonly used by great coaches in long jump development for years and are not necessarily scientifically backed. It was therefore my goal to justify some current coaching practices using research and credible scientific literature to create the ultimate guide for the development of a horizontal jumper.

1

INTRODUCTION

An introduction to the Long Jump and Triple Jump including history, the events today and thoughts for the future

Nick Newman
The Horizontal Jumps: Planning for Long Term Development

CHAPTER 1

INTRODUCTION

Track and field is the ultimate athletic discipline. It is an international sport which has existed for centuries. Thousands of coaches and athletes have come and gone, some leaving their imprint for future generations and some disappearing quietly with their knowledge shared only with a close few.

Jumping embodies much technical mastery upon which hours of repetition, video analysis and imagery are involved. It is a science unto itself, dominated by different theories and practices performed all over the world, to achieve the same elusive goals. There is no hiding in track and field, no standing in the background behind teammates or sitting on the bench because of sub-par performances. It is one man or woman alone against all other competitors.

Situations arise on a daily basis which can often make you question the very principles and underlying beliefs to which you aspire. The saying, "leave it all out on the field," echoes never truer than in this sport.

The story is often told by numbers and statistics, under which a different interpretation always lies. In this sport physical preparation, effort and sacrifice cannot be ignored due to a greater level of skill.

Physical readiness is what this sport is about. It takes hours upon hours of work spent in the weight room, on the track, in the training room, all locked in a mindset, frequently requiring much soul searching. There are rarely chances to cut corners,

Illegal and unethical actions have been well documented throughout the last 10 years, but only by a desperate few. This sport is anything but easy. In essence, we are developing our bodies and minds to perform tasks they should not actually be performing.

The sacrifice and dedication of elite track and field athletes should never be overlooked. In a word, it is remarkable. The sport becomes a life unto itself, something alive inside of you. It reminds you every second that you are a track athlete, and when handled correctly it can give you a tremendous sense of wellbeing and direction.

Why the horizontal jumps? This is my fire, my purpose, if you will. To me the long jump specifically embodies everything I ever loved about athletic greatness. The single-minded pursuit of excellence and the "me against the world" mentality creates a personal endeavor which intrinsically drives the athlete to master this masterless discipline. It encompasses all the key elements of what is deemed as athletic.

The need for great speed is paramount at the very highest level. High levels of a variety of different strength components are also needed. A high level of power is a vital element of both jumping events as well.

On top of these, other athletic abilities are also required including flexibly, coordination, visual perception, body awareness, mental toughness and more. This discipline is the complete package.

To the naked eye, the horizontal jumps can be anything from graceful to something of athletic ruggedness. It seems simple and sometimes effortless, yet can only be fully appreciated by those who have experienced it firsthand.

ABOUT THE LONG JUMP

Female long jumper in 1902

The author jumping in 2012

The long jump is one of the most popular and spectacular disciplines in track and field. The aim of the competitors is to sprint down a runway and jump off one leg from a takeoff board situated one to four meters before a perfectly leveled sand pit.

As the name of the discipline would suggest, the goal of the long jump is to jump as far into the sand as possible. In order for long jumpers to achieve maximal distance they must jump at a high speed. This speed must be reached on the runway, which is usually up to 55m in length. At the end of the runway is the takeoff board. Jump distance is measured from the edge of the takeoff board to the point of indentation the jumper makes in the sand that is closest to the takeoff board.

The takeoff board is a critical component of the long jump as it is responsible for legal and illegal jumps. The board has two parts to it. The first white section of the board is where the athlete aims to hit and is the legal section of the board.

Just after the white section is a smaller black section which is deemed the illegal part of the board and is known as the foul line. If any of the athlete's foot goes over the white and onto the foul line the jump will not count in the competition. The athlete can take off from anywhere before the board but the jump will only be measured from the legal part of the takeoff board.

Each competitor gets a preset number of jumps in a competition. The number ranges from three to six jumps after which the furthest jump from each competitor will count toward the final result.

For outdoor competitions a wind element is also considered. At the midway point of the runway a wind gauge device is placed to measure the wind speed. For a legal record to count, the wind must not be faster than +2 meters per second. If the wind is over the allowable limit, the jump distance will still count for that competition but not for any kind of record.

ABOUT THE TRIPLE JUMP

The rules of the triple jump are largely similar to that of the long jump. It is performed on the same runway as the long jump and competitors are given the same amount of jumps per competition. Wind rules are also the same. There is a difference in the placement of the takeoff board. Typically the furthest board is placed 10-13 meters from the pit. During junior level or collegiate level competitions an 11 meter board can also be seen.

A board foul is the same as for the long jump. However, it is also a foul if the athlete does not complete the correct phase sequence throughout the jump. For example, if the athlete's initiation takeoff is with his/her left foot, the phase sequence has to be left, left, right. If the takeoff is with the right foot then the phase sequence has to be right, right, left. The purpose is to land the three jumps as far from the takeoff board as possible.

HISTORY OF THE EVENTS

Historically speaking, the long jump is one of the oldest disciplines in all of sports. For thousands of years people have been jumping and running. It was an event at the original Olympic Games in Ancient Greece. The longest jump ever recorded in Ancient Greek history was 7.05m by a man named Chionis.

Although the event has evolved throughout the years it has been a part of every Olympic Games for men and since the 1928 Olympics for women. The first official world record was in 1901 by Ireland's Peter O'Connor and was a jump of 7.61m. The 8 meter barrier was first broken by America's Jesse

Owens in 1935 with a jump of 8.13m. Over 75 years later that same distance would place a long jumper in the top 20 in the world rankings. A huge breakthrough in the event came in 1968 when American Bob Beamon smashed the world record by an astounding 55cm and jumped 8.90m.

Since 1968 only one man has legally jumped over 8.90m and that was the current world and American record holder Mike Powell, when he jumped 8.95m in Tokyo in 1991. In today's long jump world, 8 meters is still the magic number and if achieved will enable the male athlete to compete in the top competitions in the world. The women's long jump record of 7.52m was set by Galina Chistyakova in Leningrad in 1988. A woman capable of jumping 6.7 meters today would be considered elite.

The triple jump is also an event with ancient origins. History has traced its beginnings back to as early as 1829 B.C. As with the long jump, the triple jump was also included in the inaugural 1896 Olympic Games. Ancient triple jumping consisted of two hops and a jump and distances of close to 15.24m were recorded. Female triple jumping however wasn't introduced until the Atlanta Olympics in 1996.

In 1995 the current world records were set in Sweden. Jonathan Edwards of Great Britain set the men's record at 18.29m (60 feet) in Gothenburg, and interestingly, at the same location, Inessa Kravets jumped 15.50 (50 feet 10.5 inches) to set the women's record. During the 21st century the standard of both the men's and women's triple jumping has maintained a high but sub world record level. Each year produces a couple of high 17 meter and low 15 meter jumpers for the men and women respectively. Both world records however currently seem out of reach for any athlete.

HORIZONTAL JUMPS OF TODAY

The greatest era of both long and triple jumping was arguably between 1980 and 2000. Here we saw the emergence and dominance of the three greatest long jumpers of all time, Carl Lewis and Mike Powell of the United States, and Ivan Pedroso of Cuba. Between them, these three athletes won numerous Olympic and World Championships. Carl Lewis won a record 4 Olympic gold medals and Ivan Pedroso won 8 World titles. Mike Powell also jumped the single furthest distance in history when he set a world record of 8.95m in 1991. In the triple jump we also saw the only 18 meter jumpers in history. Most notably, Jonathan Edwards set the bar incredibly high with his world record of 18.29m set in 1995.

The 21st century has seen virtually no improvement in overall performance within the two events. The United States jumper Dwight Phillips and Panama's Irving Saladino emerged as the world leaders, but the days of athletes jumping 8.70m on a regular basis seem all but over for now.

The women's long jump is similar; 7 meter jumps are rare today. The leading jumper is American Brittney Reese who is capable of jumping 7 meters on any given day. In the men's triple jump, Phillips Idowu of Great Britain and Christian Olson of Sweden have dominated the event. Cuba has also developed multiple elite triple jumpers over the past few years. The most consistent elite female triple jumper is Cuban's Yargeris Savigne who is regularly close to the 15m mark. Recently a host of female long and triple jumpers have also emerged as some of the best in the world.

The standard of the horizontal jumps have dropped. In the long jump, an 8.10m jump will qualify a male long jumper for virtually all major championships and will almost guarantee a place in the final. For the females, a 6.60m jump will also place very high, something you wouldn't have seen 15 years ago. In the triple jump, a 17m jump for the men will place well in major meets and mid 14m jumps will place well for the women.

One can only guess the reason for this drop in performance over the last 10-20 years. With the exception of the women's triple jump which is still a new event, the horizontal jumps have not followed the progression of other events within track and field. The 100m sprint and various distance events for example have elevated overall world standards substantially throughout the early part of this century. Various reasons from doping to the financial rewards of the sprinting events could be behind the apparent lack of talent in today's jumping elite. I will not focus on this topic, however, and will instead look at it from another point of view, which is: this should be a very exciting period in the horizontal jumps for jumpers chasing the elite level all over the world.

LOOKING TO THE FUTURE

In the men's long jump, 2009 saw the longest jump since Mike Powell's world record in 1991. It was accomplished by Dwight Phillips and was recorded at 8.74m. The rivalry between Dwight Phillips and Irving Saladino has brought back some of the event's once soaring popularity. More recently, the emergence of young talents such as Marquise Goodwin, Will Claye, and Mitchell Watt have added to the excitement of the event. However, apart from those few jumpers, the majority of the world's elite still hover around the 8.00m to 8.30m standard. This invites a few newcomers each year who manage to squeak past the 8 meter barrier. Jumping much beyond 8 meters, however, is proving extremely difficult for most athletes and the event's success now firmly lies in the ability of a few elite jumpers.

The same can be said of the 7 meter barrier for the women. A couple of jumpers are capable but the majority of the top competitors still rarely jump beyond 7 meters.

2010 was very promising for the men's triple jump and brought us the furthest jump since the 18.29m world record in 1995. Frenchman Teddy Thamgo jumped a huge 17.98m in New York. American Christian Taylor and Will Claye are also very exciting young jumpers. The women's side has not been as promising. Jumping over 15 meters is a very rare feat today and great triple jumping lies with only a couple of athletes.

I believe the future of the horizontal jumps can be as bright as we are willing to make it. Relatively speaking, there are very few superstar jumpers; this can also be said about other events in track and field. However, the number of highly educated horizontal jumps coaches is even fewer. This puts potentially talented prospects at a disadvantage straightaway. I know there are hundreds if not thousands of potentially great jumpers out there who, with the correct guidance, could break onto the world scene.

The future of the event therefore lies with the education of coaches and athletes. This is the very reason why I felt the need to write this book. There is a lot of scientific research which pertains to the horizontal jumps in one way or another. The problem many coaches and athletes face is to understand how to relate the findings of such research to the long term development of performance.

This book aims to help bridge the gap between research and practically applied training for horizontal jumpers. The aim is to help bring education to the forefront of all athletes and coaches and provide a broader understanding of the event and how best to develop the athletes who partake in it.

Major Marks in the Horizontal Jumping Events

LONG JUMP	MEN	WOMEN
World Record	8.95m (1991)	7.53m (1988)
World Junior Record	8.34m (1972)	7.14m (1983)
World Youth Record	8.25m (1986)	6.91m (1981)
African Record	8.50m (2009)	7.12m (1996)
Asian Record	8.48m (2006)	7.01m (1993)
European Record	8.86m (1987)	7.52m (1988)
American Record	8.95m (1991)	7.49m (1994)
Oceania Record	8.54m (2011)	7.00m (2002)
South American Record	8.73m (2008)	7.26m (1999)

Table 1

TRIPLE JUMP	MEN	WOMEN
World Record	18.29m (1995)	15.50m (1995)
World Junior Record	17.50m (1985)	14.62m (1996)
World Youth Record	16.89m (2000)	14.57m (1997)
African Record	17.37m (2007)	15.39m (2008)
Asian Record	17.59m (2009)	15.25m (2010)
European Record	18.29m (1995)	15.50m (1995)
American Record	18.09m (1996)	15.29m (2003)
Oceania Record	17.49m (1982)	14.04m (2003)
South American Record	17.90m (2007)	14.99m (2011)

Table 1.1

TECHNICAL COMPONENTS OF THE HORIZONTAL JUMPS

A detailed look at technical models for the long and triple jump

Nick Newman
The Horizontal Jumps: Planning for Long Term Development

CHAPTER 2

TECHNICAL COMPONENTS OF THE HORIZONTAL JUMPS

In the following chapters I will discuss which physical abilities are required for elite performance and will suggest successful methods for their development. However, to reach the elite level in the horizontal jumps, the athlete needs more than just raw physical ability. This is where technique plays an important role.

To the untrained eye it may appear that the athlete simply runs and jumps into the sand. During the early stages of development this may be true, but in order to reach the elite standards in the respective jumps, certain technical mastery needs to be achieved. This chapter will discuss the complex technical aspects of both the long and the triple jump in a simple and concise manner.

THE LONG JUMP

The technical components of the long jump may be broken down into four main categories;

1. **The Approach Run**
2. **The Takeoff**
3. **The Flight**
4. **The Landing**

Each of these categories is complex and can be broken down further for more detailed explanation.

The Approach Run

The goal of the approach run is for the athlete to reach optimal takeoff speed and position just as he/she reaches the takeoff board. For this to be achieved, a consistent and effective approach rhythm needs to be developed and practiced over and over again during the course of the training year.

This section of technical development is the most important aspect of performance. Without an efficient approach run it is impossible to achieve a consistent and effective takeoff without fouling.

An effective approach run should:

- **Begin in a consistent fashion every time** – For an effective approach to be developed it must be practiced the same way every time. The rhythm and feel of the approach must become second nature to the athlete.

- **Use a check mark for the second or third stride** – This is important because fouling issues are related in large part to error during the first 3 strides. By hitting the same mark every time on the third step the athlete is controlling this section of the approach.

- **Use the same number of running strides every time** – Once the athlete/coach has established the optimum approach distance it should be practiced the same way every time. Only when the athlete improves jump distance and sprinting speed should the approach distance be extended.

- **Generally use 16–24 strides depending on level and speed of the athlete** – The best long jumpers in the world who are often the fastest generally use 20–24 strides. A world class long jumper who relies on vertical height more than horizontal speed may use 18 strides.

- **Have a gradual and relaxed acceleration** – This is very important. The goal of an approach run is to set up a successful takeoff. Therefore, it is the speed and posture at the end of the approach that is most valuable. If the athlete strains during the initial acceleration, he/she is going to be tight and fatigued at the takeoff board.

- **Reach optimal takeoff speed roughly 5 meters from the board** – Only during the final 5m should the athlete maintain speed. Until this point he/she should be gradually increasing horizontal velocity. During the final 5m the jumper begins to prepare for takeoff.

- **Use a tall running style with bouncy rhythmic strides, especially during final 10 meters** – Approach running is slightly different than track running. From the start of the approach the athlete should feel relaxed and bouncy using fully complete strides. Achieving vertical velocity at takeoff requires the athlete to be relaxed in order to achieve the elasticity needed to jump. Approach running therefore needs to appear bouncy and rhythmic rather than aggressive and maximal in effort.

- **Be extremely active vertically with faster cadence during the final 2 strides** – During the final 2 strides the athlete is preparing for vertical lift. This is as much of an action of the body as a feeling within it. Extra vertical impulse of the running strides during this section of the approach helps maintain a tall posture with extra bounce in each stride. Achieving height at takeoff is much easier when this happens.

During the final two strides:

- **The penultimate stride is longest and extremely aggressive** – In order to minimize the loss of speed caused by the need for accuracy over the final stride it is important that the penultimate stride is actively pushed upwards and onto the takeoff action.

- **The penultimate stride leg is recovered as fast as possible into an upward and forward driving motion known as the free leg swing or knee drive** – The free leg plays a large role in achieving vertical lift at takeoff. It is also key in initiating a balanced takeoff action, which is vital for an effective flight and landing phase. The free leg should remain vertical and straight while driving upwards and out toward the pit. The knee should not be raised above parallel before the takeoff foot has left the board.

- **Upon the forward push of the penultimate stride leg onto the takeoff stride, the hips are lowered and immediately raised as the takeoff foot strikes the board** – Commonly known as gathering, this action is often performed incorrectly. Premature gathering or lowing of the hips will result in speed loss which is detrimental to the jump. If the hips are lowered too much it will also result in posture which will not favor the takeoff action. The correct gathering action is very subtle and not always visible in real speed. The most important aspect of gathering is the rise of the hips onto the takeoff action. This becomes essential for achieving vertical lift.

The Takeoff

There are many different viewpoints on how the takeoff should be performed. As a jumper and as a coach I can say I have tried them all. I will detail the takeoff style that I believe to be the most successful and is transferable to athletes with varying physical strengths and weaknesses.

The goal of the takeoff is to enable the athlete to achieve the optimum ratio of speed and height into the pit.

Good long jumping generally demonstrates a 2:1 proportion of horizontal to vertical takeoff speed. Although achieving the goal of the takeoff is largely determined by the speed and strength of the athlete, it is also affected by the correct body position and specifically the placement of the takeoff foot during takeoff.

Figure 2

The above picture demonstrates a tall takeoff action with a parallel knee drive and active follow through of the takeoff leg.

An effective takeoff should:

- **Be accurate on the takeoff board** – Fouling is both a physical and mental issue. Sometimes it is caused by an error in foot placement during certain stages of the approach. Other times it is a result of trying too hard to jump far and therefore wanting every inch out of the takeoff board. Whatever the reason for fouling, it affects every jumper in the sport and prevents many talented jumpers from reaching the elite level every year.

- **Strike the board 6–12 inches ahead of the Center of Mass (COM)** – There are several opinions on this. It is accepted that there is a trade-off between height and speed. The faster the jumper is at takeoff, the lower the takeoff angle will likely be. Each jumper or coach has to understand this relationship and decide which takeoff angle is optimal for them. Deliberately altering takeoff angles is not recommended due to other technical inconsistencies this may cause. Planting the foot directly underneath the COM will maintain the highest percentage of horizontal velocity but also cause a very flat jump. Planting the foot far ahead of the COM will cause a large loss in horizontal velocity but will cause large vertical lift during the jump. The optimal speed and height of takeoff will differ for individual athletes based on their ability. For most athletes however, planting the takeoff foot 6-12 inches ahead of their COM (hip) will generate the vertical lift required. This is of course dependent on several other factors such as leg strength and power capabilities as well.

- **Strike the board with a flat foot** - Stability of the takeoff foot is needed throughout takeoff. A takeoff on the ball of the foot would result in a dramatic loss of power. A heel first contact at takeoff will cause unnecessary speed loss.

- **Strike the board with an aggressive downward and backward motion** – This may seem obvious and as if it would be impossible not to do. However, many athletes do not fully complete the takeoff action. The best jumpers in the world actively strike the board with a pull and push action. This can be seen by observing the takeoff leg sweep back above the buttocks after takeoff. This cannot be seen by athletes who emphasize the downward strike only during takeoff.

- **Strike the board with a rigid leg** – Again, this is dependent on the athlete's strength and ability to absorb the force of a high speed takeoff. For a successful takeoff, the leg needs to act like a tightly coiled spring. There will, however, always be some leg bend and it is how fast and how much force is developed during the straightening action upon foot plant which largely determines jump distance. If the leg bends too much or is extended (straightened) too slowly, dramatic speed and power loss will result.

- **Leave contact with the board as far behind the COM as possible (T/O angle = 18-24 degrees)** – This is difficult to achieve at high speeds. It is important for achieving better takeoff angles. Lesser jumpers tend to struggle with this and as a result produce very steep takeoff angles. Remember, leaving the board when the hips are 2 feet past it will basically subtract 2 feet of actual jump distance. Add that to an effective landing and you may only need to actually jump 23 feet to register a 27 foot jump.

- **Include an aggressive free leg motion which drives up and out as fast as possible** – The free leg will aid upward momentum as well as a balanced takeoff. Often, balance of the flight is determined by the effectiveness of the free leg. Is it important that the free leg drive forward and upward and not across the body which is commonly seen.

- **Drive the opposite arm to takeoff leg upwards in sequence with the free leg** – The arms should always act in opposing sequence with the legs. This is no different at takeoff. Achieving this will result in a complete takeoff action.

The Flight

The goal of the flight phase is to prolong air time and achieve optimal position for landing. For this, an upright posture must be maintained throughout the flight to avoid over rotation and the premature dropping of the feet.

There are various styles of flight which have been discussed and debated for some time. I am an advocate of the hitch kick style simply because I believe it is natural to continue the cycling motion of the arms and legs.

Whether the hang, hitch or sail technique is natural for the athlete it is the approach, takeoff and landing which will determine jump distance. If those three components of technique are performed correctly, the flight mechanics or style of the athlete does not matter.

In general, an effective flight should:

- **Maintain an upright torso position** – Important because if the torso and chest leans forward during flight the legs will drop early forcing a premature landing action.

- **Maintain a symmetric balance** – When the athlete loses balance during the flight phase a successful landing can not be achieved.

- **Set up an effective landing position** – This is the most important aspect of the flight. A considerable loss of jump distance can occur due to a poor landing action.

The Landing

The goal of the landing is to extend the distance of the jump through two primary means. Firstly, through correct extension and timing of the leg shoot the athlete aims to connect with the sand as far as possible ahead of his/her COM.

Secondly, once the leg shoot position is achieved, the athlete must precisely time the downward strike of the sand correctly so that buttocks and torso slide past the foot hole without prematurely marking the sand.

There is a wide variety of landing techniques among elite long jumpers. All techniques aim to achieve the same thing, however, some are definitely more effective than others. As previously stated, the most effective technique is one which extends the furthest from the COM and therefore can increase jump distance the most.

Figure 2.4 demonstrates an effective landing technique. I call this the kick out technique. Here, the athlete reaches his feet as far in front of his COM as possible and makes contact the sand with his heels while maintaining straight legs for extra reach distance.

To add extra length to his leg shoot, he shifts his hips forward when he reaches the top of his jump. He then pulls his torso and buttocks past his foot mark by using his hamstrings and a forward arm swing. This is a very active landing technique and requires great timing and coordination.

Perhaps the most common landing technique is the squat landing. Both Carl Lewis and Dwight Phillips are good examples of this technique. This technique is a safe option for those who find the kick out technique difficult to master.

The squat landing is not as effective at extending the legs past the COM as the kick out technique and therefore should not be the model for athletes to follow. I am sure Carl Lewis could have jumped past 9 meters if he had landed his jumps like Mike Powell landed his own world record jump.

In general, an effective landing should:

- **Maintain an upright torso throughout** – This gives the athlete the best chance of maintaining balance and reaching the hips and feet forward of the COM.

- **Extend the feet as far past the COM as possible** – This gives the athlete the chance to maximize the distance of the jump.

- **Ensure the torso and buttocks land past the foot whole in the sand** - If the heels reach far forward of the COM but the rest of the body hits the sand prematurely the jump distance will drastically decrease.

The Long Jump Picture Guide

Figure 2.1 - Above: 2012

Figure 2.2 - Below: 1896

The Horizontal Jumps

Figure 2.3

Figure 2.4

THE TRIPLE JUMP

Although training for the two horizontal jumps is very similar, the technical execution of them is quite different. This section will focus on the technical aspect of the initial takeoff and subsequent phases of the triple jump.

The technical components of the triple jump can be broken down into 5 main categories:

1. **The Approach**
2. **The Hop Phase**
3. **The Step Phase**
4. **The Jump Phase**
5. **The Landing Phase**

The approach phase (except the final 2 strides) and the landing phase are the same as those written in the long jump technical guide in the previous section of this chapter.

During the final two strides of the approach:

- **The athlete should continue normal sprinting mechanics if using a single arm takeoff** – Maintaining all speed through the board is vital for triple jump success. As there is no need to achieve height during the initial takeoff the athlete will not lower his/her hips during the final 2 strides. Tall rhythmic sprinting through the board is needed.

- **The athlete should maintain lower limb mechanics and initiate the double arm swing if using the double arm takeoff** - If the athlete performs the double arm takeoff (highlighted later in this section), he/she will begin this motion during this stage of the approach. Before the final stride both arms will swing backward, preparing for the forward swing which will occur during takeoff.

The Initial Takeoff and Hop Phase

The triple jump differs from the long jump in the sense that the aim of the initial takeoff is only to maintain speed and NOT to produce height.

To achieve this, the angle of the hop takeoff is the same as a normal sprinting stride.

An effective initial takeoff should:

- **Maintain neutral alignment of the head, spine and hips** – Posture is very important throughout the triple jump. Natural postural alignment will help maintain balance and coordination as well as aid important displacement requirements during the jump.

- **Strike the board directly underneath or slightly ahead of the hips** – Maintaining speed throughout each phase is vital to achieving great distance with the triple jump. If the ground contact is too far in front of the hip, the athlete will lose too much speed and gain unnecessary height.

- **Strike board with a flat foot and straight leg** – Too achieve the power needed during each phase, the ground contact must be made with full surface area of the foot. Stability of the contact is also very important. As mentioned with the long jump takeoff, a straight leg is essential for maintaining speed and power.

- **Leave contact with the board as far behind the hips as possible** – This will help produce the correct takeoff angle. The first phase of the triple jump wants to maintain as much speed as possible and therefore demonstrates the lowest takeoff angle of the 3 phases.

- **Display a very active swinging free leg similar to a long jump takeoff** – A properly executed free leg helps propel the body forward and maintain horizontal velocity.

- **Display either a single or double arm motion** – Both arm styles are acceptable and have been successfully used by many elite jumpers. The single arm action promotes aggressive alternated swinging of the arms throughout the phase. For example, if the right knee is driving forward, the left arm is driven forward in sequence. The double arm action involves the backward and forward swinging action of both arms together prior to and throughout each phase.

Directly after the athlete leaves the board during the initial takeoff he/she will perform the hop phase. Here the athlete will be landing back onto his initial takeoff leg and immediately rebounding into the step phase.

For the hop phase to be successful the athlete must display a very active striking of the ground with a precision of foot contact placement. In order for technical mastery of this phase to be of benefit, the athlete must also display ability to deal with great force through excellent balance, coordination, strength and reactive power of lower limbs.

An effective hop phase should:

- **Maintain upright posture and balance** – As explained previously this is essential throughout the entire jump.

- **Cycle takeoff leg through a full range similar to a sprint stride** – The completion of the takeoff mechanism will create great displacement of the body. The full swinging movement during this phase helps achieve greater force for the step takeoff.

- **Cycle the free leg from a parallel to straight leg position prior to landing the hop** – Essential for conserving pelvic posture and preventing over rotation.

- **Make contact during hop landing slightly ahead of the hips with a flat foot** – Speed maintenance is still vital at this point but with each phase of the jump comes the need for slightly more height. A ground contact slightly farther ahead of the hips than during the initial takeoff is sufficient during this phase.

- **Prepare for step takeoff prior to hop landing with proper arm swing** – Prior to the ground contact of the step takeoff the athlete should prepare the arm swing (double or single). The timing of all swinging movements is vital during all phases of the triple jump.

- **Step takeoff should leave the ground as far behind hips as possible** – As previously discussed, great displacement of the body during all takeoffs is important for optimizing distance.

The Step Phase

The step phase is the most difficult phase to master for most triple jumpers. This phase determines the great jumpers from the average ones.

The majority of the problems associated with the step phase are related to posture and specifically forward rotation of the pelvis. Many jumpers also try to extend the phases by reaching too far upon ground contact.

Producing a good step is largely determined by how much speed the athlete has maintained throughout the previous phase. As with the hop, a good step is also dependent on the strength and reactive power of the athlete.

From a technical perspective the most important aspect of the step is what happens during the step takeoff. The need for height during the step is greater than the hop and therefore the ground strike during takeoff needs to be slighter farther ahead of the hips. A large displacement of the body past the foot strike is needed to ensure correct takeoff angle is produced.

An effective step phase should:

- Display greater height than the hop phase
- Display an active free leg swing to parallel position
- Maintain an upright posture with correct alignment
- Set up an effective jump phase

As previously discussed, the technical aspect of jump phase is identical to that of the long jump. However, you do not typically see a hitch kick flight during this phase simply because there is not enough time in the air to complete it. Other aspects are the same.

Discussed throughout this chapter are the technical components of the long and triple jump. The correct execution of these technical components is essential in providing the link between physical ability and event performance.

Away from actual jump sessions where full jumps are performed from short approaches, there are many other opportunities for technical development during training.

Technique must be stressed and practiced over and over again throughout the training year in some capacity. The coach/athlete should aim to connect various drills and exercises away from the pit with specific technical aspects of the jumps.

For example, power skip exercises used for developing leg power should also stress the parallel knee drive and hip displacement needed during the long jump takeoff.

When the athlete is performing a hopping drill for ankle strength and power development, he/she should also be cueing the correct heel-toe action seen during the triple jump phases. There are many other examples of how physical training tools should also be used for technical drilling.

Figure 2.5

The above picture demonstrates the step phase through to the landing phase. Notice the parallel knee drive during the step phase.

You can also see how the knee is driven directly forward with the toe up. This keeps all momentum going toward the pit and sets up the subsequent heel-toe contact during the jump phase.

It is also important to note the aggressive use of the arms during all phases of the triple jump.

Figure 2.6

The side view picture shows another perspective of the triple jump. Notice the final foot plant being ahead of the COM. This foot contact is farther ahead of the hip than the other phases because more height is needed during the final phase.

The table below shows how important exercises and drills used during training for the horizontal jumps can be linked with specific technical aspects of the jumps. Is it important that the athlete think about the technical cues and understand the importance of performing them correctly.

Common Exercises and Technical Cues

Exercise/Drill	Technical Cue
Power Clean	- Minimal knee bend during catch – As with support leg at takeoff - Hip/knee/ankle extension after catch – As with support leg at takeoff
Hopping	- Heel-toe foot contact – Active foot strike during LJ & TJ takeoff
Bounding	- Active knee drive – As with free leg during takeoff - Large hip displacement – As with LJ & TJ takeoff - Correct posture – As with all phases of the jumps
Skipping	- Active knee drive – As with free leg during takeoff - Large hip displacement – As with LJ & TJ takeoff - Correct posture – As with all phases of the jumps
Sprinting	- Always related to approach running rhythm and technique
Depth Jumping	- Visualize takeoff impulse during foot contacts - Short foot contact times – as with takeoff
Tempo Running	- Tall rhythmic running – As with approach and takeoff - Gradual acceleration rhythm – As with approach
Power Clean	- Minimal knee bend during catch – As with support leg at takeoff - Hip/knee/ankle extension after catch – As with support leg at takeoff

Table 2.7

Common Technical Faults & Causes

Common Faults	Event	Causes
Inconsistent approach rhythm	Long/ Triple	1. Too fast in the beginning strides 2. Irregular early stride length
Speed loss during final 3 strides	Long/ Triple	1. Excessive lowering of hips 2. Over steering to the board 3. Incorrect approach rhythm
Speed loss during takeoff	Long/ Triple	1. Excessive lowering of hips 2. Over striding the penultimate 3. Over reaching at takeoff
Takeoff (T/O) trajectory too low	Long	1. Excessive bending of T/O leg 2. T/O plant under the hips 3. Poor timing of free leg drive
Free leg driving across the body	Long	1. Wide penultimate step 2. Incorrect opposite arm drive 3. Excessive hop rotation
Over rotation during flight	Long/ Triple	1. Poor takeoff position 2. Poor timing of swinging movements 3. Poor torso position
Premature leg drop during landing	Long/ Triple	1. Over rotation during flight 2. Poor timing/ coordination 3. Sideward lean during flight
Too much height during hop phase	Triple	1. Board plant in front of hips 2. Exaggerated lowering during penultimate stride 3. Insufficient forward knee drive
Inadequate Step phase	Triple	1. Poor body position off the hop 2. Insufficient eccentric leg strength 3. Foot plant not ahead of hips
Short jump phase	Triple	1. Insufficient approach speed 2. Too much height during previous phases 3. Poor body position during jump
Excessive speed loss during phases	Triple	1. Poor foot plant positions 2. Poor use of swinging movements 3. Poor body position throughout phases
Phase distribution not optimal	Triple	1. Excessive approach speed 2. Excessive hop distance 3. Excessive height during jump

Table 2.8

NEEDS ASSESSMENT FOR THE HORIZONTAL JUMPS

A detailed look into the physical requirements needed to be horizontal jumper

Nick Newman
The Horizontal Jumps: Planning for Long Term Development

CHAPTER 3

NEEDS ASSESSMENT FOR THE HORIZONTAL JUMPS

The diagram below shows the relationship between the most important physical abilities responsible for horizontal jumping distance.

This chapter will assess the individual training requirements needed to develop these physical abilities.

The aim of this section is not to overload the reader with scientific data and reasoning but to provide the coach or athlete with facts and successful methods for developing a horizontal jumper.

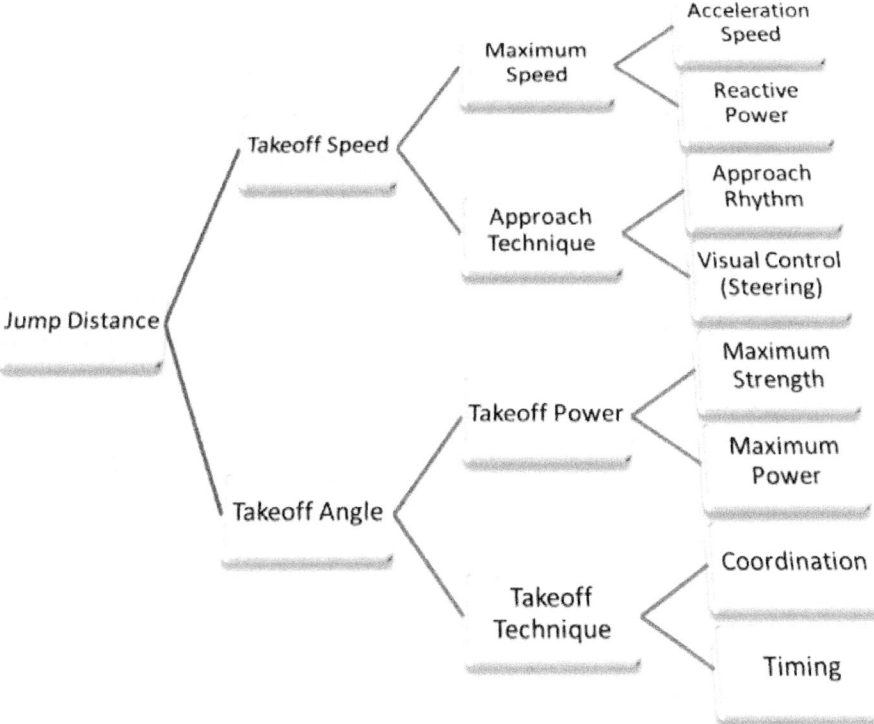

Figure 3

The Horizontal Jumps

The long jump and the triple jump are very complex events. It is commonly thought that all talented sprinters would make good jumpers simply because they are fast. This however is not the case and speed alone will not greatly benefit you in these events.

Each of the motor abilities, also called *bio-motors*, discussed in this section play an important role. It is the combination of abilities which make the best jumpers. Each bio-motor works with another and therefore all require considerable training emphasis.

The greatest jumpers in theory are those who possess very high levels of all the important abilities and who are able to use them in the correct way and at the correct time. All athletes will of course possess varying levels of these abilities.

This does not mean that if an athlete is already strong that the training program should not include strength training or if they are fast they shouldn't spend time sprinting. In these cases, there may be less emphasis placed on certain abilities and more on others. As I will discuss in more detail later on, some of the abilities needed are far easier to develop than others.

It is rare to see an athlete develop all abilities at the same rate. It is also common to see athletes struggle to develop their ability beyond a certain point. This is where the combination of specific abilities becomes very important.

As with both horizontal jumping events, there are multiple ways to jump similar distances and therefore coaches and athletes who struggle in a particular area of training should not be totally discouraged.

Although the horizontal jumps are primarily speed events, it may be surprising to know how fast most elite jumpers are actually running during their approach; certainly nowhere near the speeds you see during an elite 100m race are being reached during the approach run.

So although pure speed is hard to develop in unnaturally fast athletes, speed needed for the long and triple jump is very attainable from hard work and an effective training programs.

There are various types of elite long jumpers. Here are some examples of types of jumpers who are all capable of jumping an elite distance. There are other slight variations but those shown below are most commonly found when analyzing elite jumpers.

1. **Those who possess great speed, great power and have great technique.** These athletes are rare and are the special ones. They win gold medals and challenge world records.

2. **Those who possess great speed, average power and great technique.** These athletes can jump far and are above average elite jumpers. Their jumps often look flat but their great technique helps them achieve big distances.

3. **Those who possess average speed, great power and average technique.** These athletes are pure jumpers and achieve spectacular height when they long jump. They can jump over 8 meters but are often inconsistent with their distances. These athletes' triple jump phases would be very big but fairly slow.

4. **Those who possess average speed, average power and great technique.** These athletes are able to maximize what they have at the board and throughout the jump. They get the absolute maximum out of their ability because of superior technique.

As explained throughout this section, being an elite horizontal jumper takes a variety of skills and physical abilities.

Athletes will have dominant abilities and less dominant abilities, all of which need to be addressed and developed accordingly.

The remaining sections of this chapter will explain in detail what is required for success within the events.

SPEED

Maximum sprinting speed is the largest determining factor behind horizontal jumping distance in the long jump. The aim of a long jump training program must be centered upon improving maximal sprinting speed.

Although elite long jumpers do not necessarily take off at maximal speed, improving this quality can give them a certain comfort zone at the board. It will enable them to take off at a fast yet comfortable speed which ensures a technically sound takeoff can also be attained.

From a physical perspective, a long jumper can never be too fast. However, an optimum takeoff speed must be assessed for each athlete. This will change according to their strength levels and type of long jumper they are. The very best long jumpers in the world are able to reach up to 97% of their maximum speed at takeoff. Lesser experienced jumpers will not be able to execute a correct takeoff at these relative speeds.

As discussed in the previous section there are a few ways of jumping far. Generally speaking however there are two types of long jumpers, a speed jumper and a strength jumper.

A speed jumper possesses great elastic qualities and can generate great force at high speeds. A strength jumper generates great force with slightly longer ground contact times and therefore needs to take off at slower speeds to achieve optimum distance.

Triple jump is similar in that speed is a very important aspect of high level performance. However, typically the speed reached during a triple approach is less than during a long jump approach. The main reason for this is due to the greater need for postural control throughout the three triple jump phases. It is more important during the triple jump to achieve the least decrease in horizontal speed throughout the three phases.

However, if the athlete does not possess the necessary power during each phase, a faster initial takeoff speed will be beneficial. Often, strength jumpers excel at static power type activities such as standing long /triple jumps, bounding from a standing start, very short sprints and short approach jumps. Speed jumpers tend to excel at power tests which are performed at high speeds such as longer approach jumps, speed bounding and maximum velocity sprinting.

Speed development for a horizontal jumper consists of three key parts. Short acceleration is developed first, followed by maximum velocity speed and then speed endurance. The reason for this order is simple. In order for the athlete to reach maximal speed, a solid foundation of acceleration work needs to be performed. This is for a variety of reasons. The most important developmental reason is the need for mechanical efficiency.

To maximize physical ability the athlete must learn to move from a stationary start to high speeds quickly and efficiently with minimal wasted movements and energy.

Efficiency here will help generate the correct angles and posture needed to transition into maximal velocity sprinting. Once maximal speed has been developed we can then develop the ability to maintain speed for as long as possible. This is called *speed endurance*.

Although speed endurance is not a major requirement for the horizontal jump, it should be developed for a few reasons. Firstly it is logical to think that the longer an athlete can hold maximum speed, the more comfortable he or she will be when maintaining sub maximum speed while on the runway. Another important reason is mechanics.

Typically, speed endurance training sessions provide a practice for rhythmic and relaxed sprinting which is a very important requirement for a successful approach run. Anecdotal evidence suggests that when a jumper's speed endurance is at a high level they are ready to jump far. This could be because speed endurance develops both maximum speed and elasticity which are essential for horizontal jump performance.

STRENGTH

As discussed earlier, the most important training component for a horizontal jumper and greatest determinant of horizontal distance is maximum sprinting speed.

Therefore, the training program for such athletes should focus primarily on the development of speed.

However, a fast athlete who is not able to convert his/her speed into vertical lift during takeoff will not be a successful long jumper.

Likewise, a triple jumper who collapses during each phase will also struggle. It is therefore during takeoff where strength, particularly of the ankle, knee and hip extensors, is vital to performance.

During takeoff the athlete can experience over 1,000 pounds of force which places huge stress on the bones, joints and muscles.

For an optimum takeoff, the support leg needs to remain rigid throughout and keep any bending to a minimum. This clearly requires high levels of strength which makes this component of training very important.

Closely related to strength is the requirement of power, which is also essential for achieving optimum jump performance. An athlete needs to produce great force at takeoff in order to achieve height and/or horizontal distance.

The development of strength and particularly maximal strength greatly influences force production and the ability to tolerate the high stress which is experienced throughout training and competing in the horizontal jumps.

Strength training also provides the body with additional stimulus to recruit and develop fast twitch muscle fibers, key physiological aspects of the central nervous system, and the strength of bones and connective tissues.

A successful strength training program for a jumper must adhere to several principles including the following:

- Develop the muscle groups required for event performance

- Develop the energy systems required for event performance

- Be progressive during the long-term plan

- Develop all strength components together with varying emphasis throughout the year

- Compliment other aspects of the training program

- Continually develop assistive and secondary muscle groups throughout the year

SPECIFIC STRENGTH

I define specific strength as the ability to produce maximum force in minimal time. It is the most important strength quality associated with the horizontal jumps and is directly associated with sprinting speed and takeoff ability.

One of the most difficult elements for most jumpers is producing the force needed for optimal distance in the short time period experienced during takeoff, roughly 0.10-0.15 of a second.

This is commonly seen when jumpers transition from short approach jumps in practice to full approach jumps in competitions.

During the long jump for example, it is common to see an athlete jump 7.20m from a slower 14 stride approach. During this run the athlete will often achieve good height and produce great force during takeoff.

However, the same athlete who expects to jump 7.80m from his 20 stride approach instead jumps 7.40m and does not understand why. Assuming the athlete executed a poor full approach jump with no drastic change in technique, most of the time the reason for this sub-par performance is because the full approach requires a much faster takeoff and the athlete cannot produce enough force at this speed.

This creates an immediate problem. There is much less time during takeoff to produce the same or greater power than from 14 strides or fewer.

In addition to this, the support leg is now under greater stress and more difficult to keep stiff throughout takeoff.

The result is a far from optimal jump mainly due to the athlete's inability to produce enough force in such a limited time. This specific ability is called *rate of force development* (RFD) and along with maximal power and reactive power are the primary focus of a jumper's training program.

Power training by definition is fast and explosive. It has many advantages for athletes who train using specific power methods.

Power training develops the nervous system and these neural changes promote the muscles to achieve greater performance during fast explosive activities such as sprinting and jumping.

Large and strong muscles which do not have the ability to produce high speed force are useless for speed/power athletes.

This type of training is very effective and needs constant and consistent attention throughout the training year. This is because adaptations to the nervous system take a long time and without consistent stimulus specific adaptations will be lost.

During the training year, power development is a constant theme but it will be emphasized a lot more after the development of maximal strength.

During this time and as the competitive season approaches, it is important for energy to be reserved strictly for event-specific power development as it becomes very taxing on the body. Extra rest and recovery strategies during this time should be implemented.

The following sections are important aspects of power and performance qualities related to power which a horizontal jumper should focus upon.

MAXIMAL POWER

The jumper who produces the greatest amount of force during takeoff has the best chance of transferring sprinting speed into vertical lift. It is common to see athletes who possess great sprinting speed and yet are unable to produce high levels of force during single or multiple takeoffs.

A combination of these two abilities is needed to reach high performance in the horizontal jumps. Increasing maximum power output is therefore an important aspect of training which requires specific attention throughout the training year.

RATE OF FORCE DEVELOPMENT

Rate of force development (RFD) is the rate at which the muscles and tendons can generate force. It is not primarily developed through heavy weight training. The need for heavy weight training is linked with the goal of building a bigger engine within the body.

The idea is that if an athlete can lift more weight he or she will also be able to lift more weight quickly. A bigger more efficient engine (efficient central nervous system and muscles) can operate bigger and more efficient parts and therefore has the potential to produce more power and also produce it quicker.

A high base of maximum strength can obviously have great effects on the ability to produce maximal force. However, if RFD ability is not developed through specific means, highly developed maximal strength will not enhance this ability and may actually hinder it.

The best methods of developing RFD are ballistic weight training, heavy combined with light weight training, and other explosive movements with lighter loads such as jump takeoffs and other plyometric activities.

REACTIVE POWER

Another vital component of specific strength is called *reactive power*. This is the ability of the body to tolerate high stretch loads and the efficiency of the stretch shortening cycle.

When a muscle or tendon is stretched (lengthened) it causes a recoil effect which generates stored energy that can be used during the subsequent shortening of the muscle to develop power. The time between the lengthening and shortening of the muscle is called the *coupling phase*.

A more efficient coupling phase is most effective for generating reactive strength and is therefore the primary focus during reactive power training. Important methods for developing reactive power include plyometric exercises such as depth jumps, bounding and other variations of fast explosive movements which require a coupling phase.

Sprinting also develops the stretch shortening cycle and central nervous system, however it is not commonly known as a plyometric exercise.

GENERAL FITNESS COMPONENTS

1. **Flexibility**

Flexibility is certainly an important aspect of the training program. Flexibility should be addressed every day in one form or another. Static and dynamic stretching is included in every warm-up and cool down routine. Other forms of flexibility are also developed during hurdle walk over routines which are detailed during the training inventory page.

These exercises are used for hip mobility and flexibility, general coordination, and strengthening of the hip musculature. Flexibility of the hip extensors, hamstrings, and quadriceps are particularly important for sprinting and jumping performance.

2. Coordination

Coordination is another important general component for performance. Jumping at high speed is a very complex skill which requires coordination of a very high degree. Repetition of complex movements such as jumping and sprinting is the key to improving overall technical coordination. Sprint drills, hurdle drills, complex bounding movements and slower speed technical runs and jumps will aid the development of specific coordination.

3. Work Capacity

Work capacity is how the body is able to perform work at varying intensities and durations over a long period of time. As work capacity increases so can the volume of high intensity training performed and thus greater adaptations to training can be achieved. Work capacity generally improves year to year through carefully planned training progressions and increases in volume and intensity

4. Endurance

General endurance is not high on the priority list for a jumper. During early preparation we will touch upon it to prepare the body for a higher volume of training again after the restoration period. Training to improve general endurance will not be included in the training program during specific or competition phases.

SPECIFIC TESTING PROTOCOLS AND STANDARDS

As previously described, there are many physical factors which are needed for elite performance in the horizontal jumps. All training variations within the program are designed to improve one or more of these physical abilities. To ensure the training is having the desired effect, it is important to frequently assess the athlete's physical performance. However, although the actual event is the most important test to determine the "actual shape" of the athlete, it is not the best way to assess development during the preparation phases of the training plan.

Each training phase leading up to competitions emphasizes the development of specific abilities. Therefore, it is important that the testing protocols used match the training emphasis of that phase and progress with the training plan. There is of course some crossover from phase to phase with certain tests. This is to track the progress of particularly important tests throughout the entire preparation period.

An example of the changes in testing importance during the year is shown in the table below:

General Preparation	Specific conditioning	Technical	Competition
Standing long jump 4 Bounds + Jump 30m sprint 10 stride jump	Standing triple jump 4BJ w/4 stride run 30m sprint 12 stride jump	Fly 10m sprint 6m-1m approach speed 150m sprint Max 4B+J 14-16 stride jump	Full approach jump 6m-1m approach speed

Table 3.1

Typically, testing will take place during the unload week(s) of a training phase. This is to ensure the athlete is relatively fresh and rested from the previous hard training weeks and can perform at a high level. Training volume during the unload week is very low with the focus being placed only on a few tests and mostly on recovery.

It is important that the structure of the unload weeks remain consistent for the reliability of the tests to remain high. The important tests are to be placed toward the middle and end of unload week as this is when the athlete is most recovered from the previous 2 weeks of training and therefore the best performances can occur.

The FREELAP Timing System

During testing weeks it is vital that all evaluations are performed as precisely and consistently as possible. Using an electronic timing system to measure speed is an important way to ensure this. Not long ago it was a rare luxury to see let alone be able to use such a timing devise. Most electronic systems cost a couple of thousand dollars or more and were difficult to set up and transport around.

Early in 2011 I was introduced to the FREELAP timing System with high hopes of this changing. I was not disappointed. The cost and size of the FREELAP was a quarter of that of rival systems making it easy to use and transport to and from training. I even took it to Europe with me sliding it inside a pair of shoes within my suite case.

The FREELAP works similar to other timing systems. It has timing gates or sensors, a watch detailing times and splits and different starting equipment depending on your method for using it. As shown with the specific tests in the following section a horizontal jumper with mostly use the FREELAP for short range fly sprints and sprints between 30-150m. It can however be used to time bounding drills, short approach jump attempts and other specific exercises.

Overall the FREELAP is an excellent way of keeping track of your athlete's progress during training and testing sessions. It also helps create a competition-type intensity during training sessions and when competition season is near this edge can make a huge difference to performance.

TEST DESCRIPTIONS

1. 30m sprint

This test of acceleration ability is a good assessment of how early season sprinting development has progressed. There are many variations of this test with multiple starting and timing available.

For a jumper I recommend starting the test from an upright/2 point stance similar to how a long or triple jump approach is started. Timing methods depend on the equipment which is available. The ideal timing method would be to use FREELAP Timing system. The FREELAP option provides highly accurate timing at a moderate cost. This system can be a daily part of training as it is very lightweight and easy to transport around.

The other timing method I recommend is a much cheaper option. You will need a small stopwatch and a set of cones. The timer can be either the athlete or the coach but should remain consistent throughout the season. In this case the athlete holds the stopwatch firmly in his hand and starts it on the first foot contact past the start line. The clock is stopped as he/she passes the finish line. In my experience this testing method is very reliable and perfectly acceptable for assessing acceleration improvement.

2. Fly 10m sprint

This test assesses the top speed of the athlete and becomes increasingly important as the competitive season becomes close. Preferably this test is timed using timing sensors placed at hip height 10 meters apart. The athlete will use a 30m-40m gradual acceleration into the 10m sprint zone. The exact length of the gradual acceleration depends on the athlete's approach length ability to reach top speed. Hand timing can be used by the athlete but is less reliable than the 30m hand timing method.

3. 150m sprint

This test assesses the speed endurance of the athlete and is timed the same as the 30m test but over 150 meters.

4. Standing Long Jump (SLJ)

This test is used for the same purpose as the standing vertical jump but has more specific implications for horizontal jumpers. The athlete will stand at the end of the runway and jump off 2 feet into the sand pit. Measurements are the same as in a competition.

5. Standing Triple Jump (STJ)

This test is used for assessing unilateral reactive power at slightly higher speeds. The athlete starts with 2 feet together and performs a normal hop step and jump into the sand pit. Measurements are the same as in a competition.

6. 4 Bounds and a Jump (4BJ & M4BJ)

This is another test for unilateral reactive power but is performed at slightly higher speeds than the standing triple jump. This test is performed using a one foot forward start.

For example, with the left foot forward the athlete will jump to his right foot, then left, then right, then left and land into the sand pit. As speed power becomes the training emphasis closer to competitions, this test will progress to a maximum of 4 bounds and a jump. Here the athlete will sprint 8 total strides before the initial takeoff.

It is important to understand the relationship between the two tests. More important for a horizontal jumper than a long standing 4 B+J is the differential between the standing and the maximum test. A differential of 4.5 meters or more is outstanding and signifies a very high level of reactive power.

7. Short approach Long Jump (LJ)

This test is the most event-specific test we perform. Inline with the progression of training emphasis the short approach jump test also progresses from strength jumping to speed jumping.

I like to test from a half approach early on during strength emphasis and progress back 2-6 strides as speed and reactive power training become more predominant in the plan.

Typically for an athlete with a 20 stride full approach this would mean a 10 stride test during general prep, a 12 stride test during SPC block and a 14-16 stride test during the Technical block.

It is important to be aware that as training progresses toward a speed and power emphasis, jump distances from below 12 strides may not be as far as they were during early preparation. This is because short approach jumps below 12 strides are mostly correlated with strength gains and are not highly dependent on approach speed.

MALE TESTING STANDARDS

TEST/ LEVEL	8.00-850m 16.80-17.20m	7.50-7.99m 16.20 – 16.79m	7.10-7.49m 15.40 – 16.19	6.80-7.09m 14.60 – 15.39m
30m (electronic)	3.59 – 3.65	3.66 – 3.72	3.73 – 3.79	3.80 – 3.86
30m (hand timed)	2.90 – 3.10	3.11 – 3.20	3.21 – 3.30	3.31 – 3.40
Fly 10m	0.90 – 0.96	0.97 – 1.02	1.03 – 1.05	1.06 – 1.09
150m	15.50 – 15.90	15.91 – 16.30	16.31 – 16.60	16.61 – 17.00
SLJ	3.50m +	3.20 – 3.49m	2.90 – 3.19m	2.70 – 2.89m
STJ	10.20m +	9.80 – 10.19m	9.40 – 9.79m	9.00 – 9.39m
4BJ	17.30m +	16.50 – 17.29m	15.80 – 16.49m	15.30 – 15.79m
M4BJ	21m +	20 – 20.99m	18.00 – 19.99	17 – 18.99m
10 stride LJ	7.20m +	6.60 – 6.99m	6.40 – 6.59m	6.10 – 6.39m
12 stride LJ	7.40m +	6.90 – 7.29m	6.60 – 6.89m	6.30 – 6.59m
14 stride LJ	7.60m +	7.10m – 7.49m	6.80 – 7.09m	6.50 – 6.79m

Table 3.2

FEMALE TESTING STANDARDS

TEST/ LEVEL	6.80-7.10m 14.60 – 15.39m	6.40- 6.79m 14.00 – 14.59m	6.10-6.39m 13.50 – 13.99m	5.50- 6.09m 12.70 – 13.49m
30m (electronic)	3.80 – 3.86	3.87 – 3.93	3.94 – 4.00	4.01 – 4.15
30m (hand timed)	3.31 – 3.40	3.41 – 3.50	3.51 – 3.70	3.71 – 3.90
Fly 10m	1.06 – 1.09	1.10 – 1.13	1.14 – 1.17	1.18 – 1.21
150m	16.61 – 17.00	17.01 – 17.40	17.41 – 17.80	17.81 – 18.20
SLJ	2.70m +	2.60 – 2.69m	2.50 – 2.59m	2.20 – 2.49m
STJ	9.10m +	8.70 – 9.09m	8.40 – 8.69m	8.00 – 8.39
4BJ	15.00m +	14.70 – 14.99m	14.30 – 14.69	13.90 – 14.29m
M4BJ	18m +	17.00 – 17.99m	16.00 – 16.99m	15.00 – 15.99m
10 stride LJ	6.20m +	5.80 – 6.19m	5.50 – 5.89m	5.00 – 5.49m
12 stride LJ	6.50m +	5.80 – 6.39m	5.60 – 5.89m	5.10 – 5.59m
14 stride LJ	6.60m +	6.00 – 6.49m	5.70 – 6.09m	5.20 – 5.69m

Table 3.3

4

TRAINING PRINCIPLES APPLIED TO THE HORIZONTAL JUMPS

A detailed look into how specific physical abilities needed for success in the horizontal jumps are developed in both the short term and the long term

Nick Newman
The Horizontal Jumps: Planning for Long Term Development

CHAPTER 4

TRAINING PRINCIPLES APPLIED TO THE HORIZONTAL JUMPS

ACCELERATION DEVELOPMENT

Acceleration development is done through various methods of repeated sprinting at 95-100% of maximum effort. The methods of acceleration development listed below are limited to the track.

Repeated sprinting methods are most successful when developing acceleration and maximum speed. However it is important to note that it is not the only method. Acceleration is highly linked with maximum strength and many other elements within the training program aid its development.

Weight training, plyometrics, and medicine ball throwing all positively affect the ability to accelerate at high speed.

The list of acceleration workouts below is not an exhaustive list and throughout the training program within this book you will notice many variations of these methods.

1. **6-8x 10-30m sprint ladder**

This drill develops stride frequency, rhythm and correct sprinting posture. Sticks are placed on the track so that the distance between each one is gradually increased to match the athlete's stride length.

The aim is to place the sticks slightly closer than the normal stride length to promote an increase in stride frequency. It also creates a stride rhythm which is very important during the long jump approach.

2. **6-8x 20m sprints**

3. **2-4x (3x30m sprints)**

4.   3x 20, 30, 40m sprints

These short acceleration workouts are performed using various starting methods and should be performed at 95% effort or more.

Typically 1 minute of recovery for every 10m sprinted is required between each sprint and the sum of repetition rest is used between sets.

For example, if the workout is 3 sets of 2 repetitions of 30m sprints, the rest between each repetition would be 3 minutes and the rest between each set would be 6 minutes.

Rest intervals may be longer for sprints over 60m in length and during the competition period of the year.

5.   3x (3x30m resisted/uphill sprints)

Resisted sprints can be performed up a slight incline or by using a parachute or a weight sled to provide the resistance. My preferred method is to use an incline hill of 2-4% grade.

Hill sprints are excellent at teaching correct acceleration posture and foot strike position.

Resisted sprints using a weighted sled are also common practice for sprinters and jumpers. It is a common mistake to load the sled so heavily the athlete struggles to pull with correct sprinting technique.

This should be avoided and it is recommended to use no more than 10-15% of the athlete's body weight as resistance. When performed correctly these methods are excellent for developing power and short sprinting ability.

Another successful method of hill/resisted sprints is to contrast the method with normal sprints within the same workout.

For example, an athlete may perform a single 20m hill sprint followed by a 20m sprint on the track. This series would be repeated 3-5 times in a workout.

Using a similar principle it is also common to combine weight training and medicine ball throwing with sprinting.

Here there are many variations. For example, a set of squats followed by a 20m sprint or a BLF medicine ball throw directly into a 20m sprint.

MAXIMUM VELOCITY DEVELOPMENT

Similar to acceleration development, specific track workouts will focus on the development of maximum sprinting speed. This quality is difficult to develop and is largely determined by genetics. It is also not as closely linked to maximum strength as is acceleration speed.

To develop maximum speed the body needs a constant speed reminder and the repetition method achieves this well. High speed plyometrics and fast repetition weight training positively impact the development of max speed.

As with all bio-motors speed development programs need constant variation and progression in order for body to continue to adapt to the training stimulus.

These workouts are very intense by nature and require a rested athlete prior to the start of the session. Full recovery between sprints is needed during all session aiming to develop true top sprinting speed.

The most common example of this sectional approach to speed development is called the *fly sprint*. Here, the athlete will gradually build his/her speed over 30-40m and sprint at maximal effort for a duration of 1-3 seconds after the buildup is complete.

The emphasis of these sessions is to have the athlete focus his/her energy on the section of the sprint that is performed at max speed. By not performing the acceleration section of the sprint prior to where max speed is reached it enables the athlete to learn to sprint relaxed and efficiently with minimal fatigue.

Some methods combine various sections of relaxed sprinting, maximal sprinting and gradual acceleration together over a longer distance. Other methods of maximum speed training combine acceleration with max speed. Most of these are listed in the speed endurance section.

The list below is only a sample selection of ways to develop maximal sprinting speed. Optimum development requires the inclusion of all training methods.

For all methods of maximal speed development it is essential that full recovery is achieved between each sprint. This is usually anywhere from 3-10 minutes.

1. **6-8x Full-approach runs**

Although approach running is primarily for technical and accuracy purposes, they do require repetitions of near maximal speed which provides a good stimulus for speed development. It is important for the athlete and coach to aim for maximal or near maximal speed to occur over the final 10m of the approach run. Contrasting approach runs with fly 10m sprints on the track during the same session works well to minimize the gap between max speed and approach speed.

2. **6-8x Fly 20m sprints w/30m build up**

Here the athlete will accelerate in a sub-max fashion and attempt to reach 95% speed at the 30m mark. The athlete will then sprint as fast as possible for 20m before gradually slowing down. This method provides the opportunity to focus on maximal running without a preceding hard acceleration. This not only allows complete focus on maximal sprinting but also uses a similar energy and acceleration pattern needed during a long jump approach run.

3. **2-4x (3x60m FSF)**

During this float-sprint-float (FSF) run the athlete will build up gradually for 20m, sprint hard for an additional 20m, and then maintain speed in a relaxed fashion over the final 20m. This will build maximal speed endurance and also teach the athlete to sprint relaxed, which is difficult but very important to learn. The length of the FSF will vary depending on the athlete's fitness and time of the training year.

4. **4x 100m SFS (Sprint Float Sprint)**

Similar to FSF, Sprint Float Sprints require the athlete to sprint hard and relax during various sections of the run. An example could be to accelerate hard for 30m, relax over 20m, sprint hard for 30m, and then relax over the final 20m.

5. **4-6x Downhill 40m sprints**

This method is extremely high intensity and should be used only with experienced and highly developed athletes. Here the athlete will reach supramaximal speeds which cannot ordinarily be attained through normal sprinting. This method can also be contrasted with normal sprinting. It is highly recommended to run several repetitions at sub-max effort before attempting maximum sprinting speed.

SPEED ENDURANCE DEVELOPMENT

Speed endurance sessions are performed the least of all sprint sessions for horizontal jumpers.

Two types of speed endurance will be developed: short and long. Short speed endurance develops the ability to perform repeated high speed sprints with minimal fatigue. Long speed endurance develops the ability to hold maximum speed over a longer duration.

These workouts are highly intense and can be very draining on the athlete. Long speed endurance is dropped completely from the program during the competition phase and is only used intermittently during the year.

Short speed endurance is used close to the competition phase to complete development of competition fitness. It will be used briefly during a long competition phase for maintenance purposes.

Below are examples of short and long speed endurance training sessions.

Short Speed Endurance

1. **3x2x 40m sprints** (2/6 min recovery)

2. **3x2x 60m sprints** (4/6 min recovery)

3. **2-4x 80m sprints** (6 min recovery)

These sprints are similar to other sprint workouts listed however in this case the recovery is less than full. These are very tough workouts and should be used minimally, mostly prior to the competition phase.

Long Speed Endurance

1. **3-6x 150m** (5 min recovery)

2. **2x 100m, 1x 150m, 1x 300m sprints** (10/12/15 min recovery)

3. **300m, 200m, 100m sprints** (12/10/8 min recovery)

From a fatigue perspective, these workouts are the hardest that a jumper will do. They are performed away from the competition block and are phased out of the program completely during the peak of the season.

COMPONENTS OF STRENGTH DEVELOPMENT
GENERAL STRENGTH

General strength, although not directly responsible for event specific performance, plays an important role in the training program. General strength is literally as the name appears. It is total body strength, including joints, bones, ligaments, tendons, and muscles that will assist the primary muscles largely responsible for event specific performance.

When general strength is at an optimal level, the ability to handle the stresses of everyday training will be high. Therefore, the development of subsequent abilities also improves and the risk of injury is kept to a minimum. General strength is always required and therefore needs to be developed throughout the entire year. As a result, it is used as a method of maintaining or developing fitness while aiding recovery during low intensity training days.

General strength development takes place through various low intensity methods. Mainly traditional callisthenic exercises, weight circuits, medicine ball movements and other light loading activities such as hopping and barefoot jogging are used during general strength training. The routines are usually performed in a circuit fashion with high repetitions including movements which address core stability, balance, foot/ankle strength, auxiliary muscle strength, and special injury prevention exercises (Table 4).

Due to the low intensity and non-specific nature of this training component, it is often the least favored part of training for jumpers and sprinters. It may therefore be beneficial to include some aspect of general strength work into the athlete's warm-up and cool down routines. As a coach, feel free to create fun and challenging routines for your athletes. Examples of various general strength routines are listed in the training inventory section of this book.

General Guidelines for General Strength Training	
Load	20-60% 1RM
Repetitions	8-20
Sets	2-4
Movement speed	Moderate/Slow
Rest	30 sec – 1 min
Frequency	4-6 per week

Table 4

MAXIMUM STRENGTH

Maximum strength can be described as the ability of the skeletal muscle to produce maximal tension or force at a given velocity. As previously stated, the ability of an athlete to produce force is a key determining factor of horizontal jump performance. It establishes the specific base for speed and power development and therefore is one of the most important training components for horizontal jumpers.

Optimal maximum strength aids speed and power development and the ability to withstand the forces which are placed on the body during sprinting and the takeoff action.

Specifically, it is the maximum eccentric strength of the quadriceps muscles which enable the support leg to remain rigid throughout takeoff.

Special attention must therefore be placed on developing eccentric leg strength and leg stiffness during the maximum strength training program.

The development of maximal strength takes place through various methods of very high-intensity weight training. During all methods it is important to comply with the principles listed below:

1. Use full range of movement to recruit the largest muscles
2. Focus on leg extensor development while keeping upper body work to a minimum
3. Keep repetitions in the 1-4 range with an intensity of 85-100% of 1RM
4. Keep frequency to 2-3 times per week and 1-2 times per week during competitions
5. Always perform after speed, power or technical training

It is important to understand the place strength training occupies in the overall training program. We do not want the weight training program to complicate the overall training plan. For a jumper we use weight training for a specific purpose which is secondary to the speed and elasticity development performed on the track through sprinting and jumping exercises. Many coaches have a tendency to use exercises and methodologies during this section of training which are overly-complicated for producing the desired results.

The primary goal of weight training earlier in the program is to develop general strength followed by maximal strength. The secondary goal is to development explosive power. This emphasis will change as the year progresses. After the initial max strength emphasis very heavy lifting will be minimally used as it the dampers elastic qualities which are primarily responsible for sprinting and jumping ability. More detail regarding the periodization of the strength training program is discussed in Chapter 5.

Described below are effective methods that can be used for developing maximal strength and explosive power in the weight room.

Maximal Load Method

This is the most common method for developing maximum strength and is highly effective for increasing strength while minimizing the increase of body weight. This method also provides an easy way to quantify and measure progressions on a regular basis.

As the name suggests, the maximum load method requires very heavy bouts of weight training. As a result, positive links with the central nervous system develop improving muscle coordination and synchronization. As with other forms of training for a jumper, this high central nervous system (CNS) activation also results in the decrease of muscular inhibition.

This basically means that consistent exposure to this training method will enable the athlete to work at a higher percentage of his/her maximum ability without restriction from various protective mechanisms within the body. As you can imagine, this factor is vital when aiming to achieve maximum power and sprinting speed.

For optimal development using the maximum load method it is important that the prime muscles responsible for horizontal jump performance are worked in this way. Due to the requirement of multiple high intensity sets it is also not possible to use many exercises per session. Focus should therefore be placed on Olympic movements and squat variations predominantly. Another important consideration while using any method of weight is the execution of the movement itself.

The aim for a long jumper is to recruit as many fast twitch muscle fibers as possible every time they train. The best to do this is to train the largest muscles at maximum intensity as often as possible.

Therefore, during every lift it is key to perform it explosively at high speeds. Realistically, when lifting 90% of a 1RM, the bar with not be moving very fast. It is therefore the effort which is most important in this case as effort also contributes along with load percentage to overall intensity.

General Guidelines for Maximal Load Method	
Load	85-100% of 1RM
Repetitions	1-4
Sets	4-8
Movement speed	Explosive/Fast
Rest	3-6 minutes
Frequency	1-3 per week

Table 4.1

Maximal Eccentric Load Method

This method of training is for experienced athletes who have already achieved a high level of maximal strength using the Maximum Load Method. This method allows for greater tension to be placed on the muscles which can elicit increased strength gains if a plateau has occurred.

A key result of this training method is the development of leg stiffness which is vital for successful takeoffs in both horizontal jumps. As previously discussed, it is here where the athlete has to overcome huge forces and maintain leg stiffness to resist buckling. Eccentric strength training enables you to resist far greater forces than you can actually lift.

During the lowering phase of an exercise (eccentric phase) muscles can produce greater muscular tension and handle up to 140% of what they lift concentrically (upward phase).

This method is not to be performed in isolation but instead along with the max load method or power type training. It is important to balance antagonist muscles using this method and not just focus on the quadriceps group for example. Due to the nature of the supra-maximal loads, the movement speed during this method is very slow. This is another reason why it is often used with fast stiff legged jumping exercises like a jump squat for example.

The key throughout this exercise is to resist for as long as possible while lowering the weight. The safety bars will be set at the parallel squat position in order to catch the bar at the end of the movement.

General Guidelines for Maximal Eccentric Load Method	
Load	100-140% of 1RM
Repetitions	1-3
Sets	4-8
Movement speed	Slow
Rest	3-6 minutes
Frequency	0-1 per week

Table 4.2

Maximal Isometric Method

Another maximal strength method which is also used in conjunction with the max load method by advanced athletes is called the *isometric method*. Here, maximal tension within the muscle at a certain joint angle is achieved through a static contraction.

A static contraction is one where the joint is fixed in one position throughout the duration of the repetition. This can be achieved by exerting force against a fixed bar or by placing enough weight on the bar so it cannot be moved. Most popular isometric exercises for jumpers include the static squat and mid thigh clean pull.

For horizontal jumpers this can have very specific requirements as maximum knee bend during takeoff usually will not exceed 130 degrees.

Therefore it is around 130 degrees of knee bend in which the bar position is set up and most successfully used. Due to the high specificity of joint angle and the method's ability to maintain maximal strength, it is suggested that this method be used during competition phase along with specific power training methods.

General Guidelines for Maximal Isometric Load Method	
Load	80-100% of 1RM
Duration of repetitions	3-8 seconds
Sets	6+
Movement speed	Max effort
Rest	3-6 minutes
Frequency	1-2 per week

Table 4.3

POWER DEVELOPMENT

Listed below are a variety of successful methods for developing explosive power in horizontal jumpers. As for the development of maximum strength, the use of specific weight training methods can also be important for developing power. As the emphasis is placed on the speed of movement during power development, the loading percentages used are of the upmost importance.

Generally speaking peak power is developed using 30-50% 1rm for squatting movements and 70-80% 1rm for Olympic lifting movements. As previously mentioned maximum strength will improve an athlete's ability to produce power. This is because as strength increases so does the ability to generate maximum force.

When combined with power training this then increases the amount of force which can be produced in shorter time periods as well. Specific weight training for power development is described below.

Speed Repetition Method

Moving an external resistance as fast as possible is a great way of developing power. This method of weight training will use similar exercises than the maximum strength program however the emphasis here is much different. The speed repetition method will be performed using two variations.

Variation A requires continuous repetitions at the highest possible speeds. Naturally the loading for this variation should be on the lower end. This addresses the need for high contraction speeds and the ability to produce fast force.

Variation B addresses the need for maximum power production and requires repetitions performed with maximum dynamic effort. Loading of a slightly higher weight is used for this variation as force production is of more importance. Slight rest periods between repetitions are necessary during variation B due to the need for full energy concentration during each repetition.

It is worth stressing again that the most important aspect of this training method is the speed of execution. This includes the initial acceleration and speed through the full range of the movement. Maximum dynamic effort must be applied during this method for maximum power to increase.

General Guidelines for the Speed Repetition Method Variation A	
Load	30-50% of 1RM
Sets	3-6
Repetitions	3-8
Movement speed	Fast & Continuous
Rest	2-6 minutes
Frequency	2-3 per week

Table 4.4

General Guidelines for the Speed Repetition Method Variation B	
Load	50-80% of 1RM
Sets	3-6
Repetitions	3-8
Movement speed	Fast & Explosive
Rest	2-6 minutes
Frequency	2-3 per week

Table 4.5

Contrast loading method

To combat any loss in maximum strength during the competitive phase when power development is the primary focus, the use of a combination of load percentages at the same time is advised.

Combining various loads of resistance within a week or training cycle can stimulate adaptation at a greater rate.

Although heavy loads are best for developing maximum strength and lighter loads are best for developing power, a combination of the two seems to work best.

As previously discussed maximum strength and power should be developed together throughout the training year. This is also the premise behind undulating periodization which is how our training system is set up.

This leads to an important training concept called *contrast load training*. The contrast load method is used by horizontal jumpers because of the importance of both strength and power to the outcome of event performance.

All training components must be planned together to ensure peak fitness of all bio-motors is reached.

Contrast loading during an individual session consists of performing alternate sets of high and low 1rm percentages.

The first set aims to recruit maximum muscle fibers and will promote strength development.

The second set aims to produce maximum speed muscle contractions and will promote power development.

General Guidelines for the Contrast Loading Method	
Strength Load	85% + of 1RM
Power Load	30-75%
Sets	3-6
Repetitions	3-8
Movement speed	Fast & Explosive
Rest	1min/super-set, 3-5 min set
Frequency	1-2 per week

Table 4.6

The weight training methods discussed above target the improvement of rate of force development which combined with an efficient stretch shortening cycle is key for high levels of power production.

Improving the stretch shortening cycle requires very fast bouts of explosive activity with minimal ground contact time. For this requirement, plyometric training is used.

This training method is most specific for developing power in sprinters and jumpers as it closely simulates the time/force requirements of the events.

Due to the importance of this training method, it is important to take the time to understand the method in more detail.

PLYOMETRIC TRAINING

Plyometrics are any exercise where the muscle is loaded or stretched eccentrically then immediately contracted concentrically. In other words, the muscle is stretched (i.e. loaded) before it is contracted. Examples of this eccentric- concentric action are very common throughout track and field.

During the long jump takeoff the explosive straightening of the support leg is preceded by an impact which bends the leg and stretches the extensor muscles. The stored energy produced during this bending (amortization) phase of the takeoff action is used to produce the explosive force needed to jump.

How does it work? When a quick stretch is detected in the muscles, an involuntary, protective response occurs to prevent overstretching and injury. This response is known as the **stretch reflex**. The stretch reflex increases the activity in the muscles undergoing the stretch or eccentric muscle action, allowing it to act much more forcefully.

The result is a powerful braking effect and the potential for a powerful concentric muscle action. If the concentric muscle action does not occur immediately after the pre-stretch, the potential energy produced by the stretch reflex response is lost. In other words, if there is a delay between the initial pre-jump and the jumping up part of a counter movement jump the effect of the recoiled energy produced during the pre-stretch will be lost.

So, to describe in more detail, all plyometric movements involve **three** phases. The first phase is the pre-stretch or eccentric muscle action. Here, elastic energy is generated and stored. The second phase is the time between the end of the pre-stretch and the start of the concentric muscle action. This brief transition period from stretching to contracting is known as the **amortization** phase.

The shorter this phase is, the more powerful the subsequent muscle contraction will be. The third and final phase is the actual muscle contraction. In practice, this is the movement the athlete desires – the powerful jump or throw. This sequence of three phases is called the ***stretch-shortening cycle***. In fact, plyometrics could also be called *stretch-shortening cycle exercises*.

* As you can imagine plyometric training is very popular among sprinters and jumpers. It is however a widely abused method of training. Certain advanced plyometric exercises which are highlighted later can be very stressful and should be used sparingly within the training program.

As a general rule plyometrics should be used in low volume 2-3 times per week. It is far more beneficial to under use this method than is it to overuse it. There are many other variables to consider when using plyometric training. These also change depending on the time of the training year and the experience and tolerance level of the athlete.

If plyometric training is not carefully prescribed and monitored it can be a very easy way to over train your athlete. Plyometric progressions should be followed by all athletes no matter their level as they provide a good physical and technical base which is important to the long term training plan. Detailed in chapter 8 are various levels of plyometric training for beginner through advanced athletes. The beginner exercises are the least intense exercises and can be prescribed in higher volumes with shorter rest periods between sets.

The advanced exercises are the highest intense exercises and are for experienced athletes with sufficient strength levels and who have progressed through all levels of plyometrics over a 2-4 year period. These exercises require few repetitions and full recovery between each set. It is important to emphasize the importance of each intensity level of plyometric exercises. Elite athletes will greatly benefit from beginner and advanced plyometrics and should gradually progress them as with any other training method.

Below is a general characterization of plyometric exercises and recommended protocols for implementing them in a training program.

Plyometric Category	Intensity Level	Sets/ Reps	Rest Interval	Phase
1. High Depth Jumps 2. Speed Bounds 3. Max Bounds	Maximum	2-4 x 4-6	6-10 min	Special Prep / Competition
1. Continuous Medium Depth Jumps 2. S/L Depth Jumps	Very High	2-4 x 4-6	4-6 min	Specific Prep / Special Prep
1. Standing Bounds 2. Standing S/L Bounds 3. Weighted Jumps	Sub Maximum	4-6 x 10-20	3-5 min	General Prep / Specific Prep / Special Prep
1. Low Box Depth Jumps 2. Stair Jumping 3. Hurdle hops	Medium	4-6 x 10-20	3-5 min	General Prep / Specific Prep / Special Prep
1. Vertical Multi Jumps 2. Medicine Ball Throws 3. Hopping	Low	4-6 x 10-20	2-3 min	General Prep / Specific Prep / Special Prep

Table 4.7

REST & RECOVERY

Rest and recovery is an essential part of the training program. Most athletes, especially full time elite's are often training multiple times per day or for extended periods of time. With this, comes a high level of physical and mental fatigue. The greater fatigue, the greater need for countermeasures against effects like lower recovery rates, poor coordination, decreased strength and power, decreased speed, and mental exhaustion leading to a variety of psychological issues.

Understanding and implementing recovery techniques before, during, and after training sessions is one of the most effective ways to prevent such decreases in performance from occurring. This chapter will briefly cover a variety of effective methods of recovery enhancement commonly used with horizontal jumpers. It will also cover important factors related to recovery such as overreaching and overtraining and how they play an important role in the development process.

Overreaching

As a coach and athlete is it essential to understand the difference between good and bad fatigue. Physical and psychological fatigue are natural responses to high intensity training. They are also vital to the supercompensation theory which basically states that after an athlete undergoes physical stress his/her performance will acutely decrease. After a period of rest and recovery his/her performance will then increase above initials levels. It is therefore the management of fatigue that becomes the most important recovery factor. Overreaching is the short term decrease in performance that occurs as a result of a hard training session or multiple sessions. It is a deliberate part of the training program and is essential for long term development.

Understanding this is important because athletes who expect to feel as they do in competitions during the entirety of preseason training will often worry and begin to question their training. It is common after a period of heavy weight training or after the highest load training phase that certain performance measures will decrease. This overreaching phase can last a few days or a few weeks depending on the length of the high load training. A single high intensity training session may see a performance decrease lasting between 24-48 hours. A 3-6 week training phase may take 2-5 weeks of tapering to truly see the performance gains. The timing of this is key and obviously the most important time for an athlete to be at his/her best is during the competition phase.

The periodized training programs in this book take full advantage of the overreaching process. Each unloading week enables the athlete to recovery and rebuild for the next training. However, a true recovery and supercompensation effect won't be seen until a longer tapering period occurs leading directly to the competition phase and throughout peaking.

Overtraining

Overtraining is certainly the enemy of high performance training. It is the long term negative effects that fatigue can have on athletic performance. Unlike with overreaching, true restoration from overtraining can take up to several months.

A well constructed training program will likely prevent overtraining from occurring. However, this is not always the case. Certain athletes who like to push everything to the max and who are generally high intense by nature are more likely to suffer overtraining than others. All athletes will benefit from physical and psychological assessments periodically. Simple questioning and basic performance tests can show a fatigued athlete.

Any training session should be change to a recovery session such as easy tempo running if an athlete is showing signs of fatigue beyond what is expected. Adjusting training in such a way and incorporating the recovery methods described later in this chapter can successfully decrease early signs of overtraining. These methods should be used for as long as it takes for the athlete to return to normal testing measures.

The list below details common symptoms of overtraining:

- Decreased performance
- Decreased motivation
- Decreased sleep quality
- Decreased appetite
- Increased resting heart rate
- Increased irritability and depression
- Increased resting blood pressure

Preventing Overtraining

A well planned training program will go a long way to avoiding overtraining. This alone however will not always guarantee overtraining doesn't occur. It is important for the coach and athlete to communicate daily and discuss the overtraining symptoms listed above.

A detailed training log describing how the athlete is feeling and performing from day to day is also highly recommended. This should also include a detailed account of training type, volume, intensity, sleep quality, and diet. A training log can greatly help an athlete and coach analyze all aspects of the program in relation to possible overtraining occurrences.

Perhaps the easiest and most important method for monitoring a overtraining is by ensuring regular testing and unloading weeks are included in the program. A dramatic decrease in training volume accompanied by specific performance tests should be issued every 3-4 weeks.

Long term stagnation or performance decreases is a key sign that overtraining may be occurring and an adjustment to the training program is immediately required.

Other simple methods for monitoring overtraining include, keeping track of diet, sleep quality, mood and motivation levels and resting heart rate upon waking up. Any long term findings which are abnormal can be a sign of overtraining.

Common Recovery Methods

The following recovery methods which shall be briefly described are commonly used among jumpers and sprinters and can help promote recovery and enhance training adaptation. As they are not my area of expertise I will describe the basics of what, when and why these methods should be used. I strongly recommend you consult a physical therapist regarding specific recovery methods and include them as part of your training program.

Passive Recovery

Sleep is essential for recovery. It is recommended that athletes get 9-10 hours of sleep per day. The majority of this should come from overnight sleep and the remaining from intermittent napping throughout the day. Short power napping of 10-15 minutes can positively improve performance.

Active Recovery

Light exercise sessions play an important role in recovery. They act as a soothing contrast to the high intensity training that the majority of the training program consists of. 10-20 minutes of light jogging after a high intense session can greatly reduce the onset of muscle soreness and aid CNS recovery. Other choices include light weight circuits and stretching routines.

Cryotherapy

The use of ice or cold treatment is very common among all athletes. Cold therapy reduces inflammation and pain but can acutely decrease performance abilities and is therefore recommended as a post-training recovery method. It is highly recommended following an acute injury and for severe muscle soreness.

Ice or cold may play an important long-term role within a program, however I suggest using it primarily for injury purposes. Ice baths should be performed for 10-20 minutes at a temperature of around 15 degrees C. Ice massage can be performed for 5-10 minutes and repeated every 20 minutes. Ice packs can be used for a period 1-2 hours using a contrast of 20 minutes on and 20 minutes off.

Thermotherapy

The use of heat is common among athletes, however very little research actually proves its purpose. It is suggested that 20 minutes of hot water immersion (around 40 degrees C) can enhance recovery. Cryotherapy is likely more beneficial for reducing muscle soreness. Using a sauna may also increase total body recovery when used 1-2 times per week for 30 minutes at a temperature of around 90 degrees C.

Massage

The use of massage techniques is very popular among athletes of all sports. Massage can be used pre-training as well as post-training. Pre-training massage acts as stimulation for the CNS and required muscles and can last between 10-15 minutes.

Post-training massage is for restoration purposes and aids relaxation and blood flow. It should be undertaken 1-2 hours following high intense training sessions. Short post-training massages of 10-20 minutes can be issued multiple times per day.

5

PERIODIZATION OF INDIVIDUAL TRAINING COMPONENTS

A detailed look into how the pieces of the puzzle are put together and progress is made throughout the training year.

Nick Newman
The Horizontal Jumps: Planning for Long Term Development

CHAPTER 5

THE PERIODIZATION OF INDIVIDUAL TRAINING COMPONENTS

Components of the training program such as strength and speed can be considered the ingredients for cooking a gourmet meal. As you can imagine, trying to cook without a recipe will easily turn into a disaster.

However, following a recipe with ingredients that have not been previously prepared would not produce a great meal either.

The periodization of these training components can therefore be looked at as the seasoning of the cooking ingredients. The seasoned ingredients can then be a part of the recipe.

In this case the recipe, or the complete periodized training program discussed in chapter 7s, is the final part of producing a successful jumper.

If the program is constructed in a successful way, both physical and technical improvements will occur with the avoidance of frequent plateaus.

This chapter focuses on how the ingredients of the program progress and are manipulated over the course of the year. With the majority of the year focused on developing specific athletics abilities, it is very easy for the athlete to become mentally and physical bored.

Physical boredom, known as *accommodation*, is when the body no longer adapts to the training stimulus. This is something all training program aim to avoid.

However, because different athletes adapt at different rates, the planning and progression of these training components can often be individually determined.

The following discusses the individual training components and how they are planned throughout the year.

WARM-UP / COOL-DOWN

The warm-up and cool-down components of the daily training routine play a very important role. They are the first and last activities performed daily.

An effective warm-up routine should enable an athlete to reach a state of training readiness, should help prevent injury, and should be designed to steadily raise core temperature and physical arousal levels throughout the routine. For a long time it was thought that jogging a few laps of the track followed by static stretching was enough to attain such performance readiness.

The current trend throughout literature suggests that jogging along with static stretching negatively affect the ability to produce speed and power. It is now commonly accepted that dynamic activities such as skipping, striding, and dynamic stretching are more beneficial for speed/power athletes during the warm-up segment of the workout. If static stretching is preferred by an athlete it is advised that he/she perform it early in the warm-up and follow it with dynamic stretching exercises.

It is recommended that the warm-up routine be broken into a general section and a specific section and to progress to more specific movements related to that day's training program. For example, after the initial general warm-up which raises heart rate and blood flow to the working muscles, an athlete performs small dynamic exercises such as lunges and squats.

The athlete then begins dynamic stretching movements. After dynamic stretching, the athlete is ready for general physical activity but probably not ready to perform explosive movements such as maximal sprints.

To ensure complete physical readiness the athlete completes the final and most specific section of the warm-up. In this case, this includes sub-maximal sprinting over short distances. The idea is to perform 3-4 sprints of gradually increasing intensity. It is worth noting that elite athletes have built a high level of work capacity over years of training. These warm-up routines may be similar to the workouts themselves for beginning athletes.

Therefore, it is very important that warm-ups are specifically designed for the athlete's needs and individual requirements. Detailed in the training inventory are various warm-up routines. The following is a general outline for the warm-up routine:

Guidelines for Sprint/Jumps Specific Warm-up

General Warm-up

- 800m skipping the straights, jogging the curves

Static Flexibility

- 6-10 exercises (Legs, Core, Arms, Shoulders, Chest etc)
- Hold for 8-12 seconds
- Repeat 2-3 times

Sprint Drills

- 6-10 drills focusing on posture, alignment, sprint mechanics
- 20-40m for each drill
- Slow walk back recovery

Dynamic Flexibility

- 6-10 exercises
- Specific range of motion should be stressed
- 8-12 dynamic stretches (bounces) per exercise

Speed Development

In general terms, the progression of speed development used throughout this program is in the following order: (1) Acceleration; (2) Max Speed; and (3) Speed Endurance.

However, these 3 aspects of speed can also be broken down further. Acceleration development from 0-30m will be a part of the program throughout the year.

During the initial stages of the program, high repetitions of very short distances are performed using a variety of starting methods. This develops the initial impulse, simulates contact times similar to that during takeoff, develops overall power and also allows for technical work to take place.

When the athlete is ready to increase acceleration distance (physically and technically) the program will progress.

The next progression is the development of maximum speed. A basic requirement of reaching maximum speed is efficient acceleration mechanics and therefore developing acceleration will remain a primary focus.

Maximum speed development will also increase in distance over time but will rarely go beyond 30m as true max speed cannot be maintained any longer than that.

The distance used during maximum speed workouts will then decrease during the competition blocks to ensure that specificity is high and fatigue is low. Speed endurance will be phased in gradually throughout preparation and will decrease in distance as competition block approaches.

During competition block, maintenance of speed endurance occurs through only a couple of fast repetitions of 60-120m sprints.

It is important to keep low volumes of speed endurance work in the program during competition block for various reasons. It helps maintain general fitness, elasticity, and general strength as well as preventing early peaking.

Repetitions of such training during this time need to be kept to a minimum to avoid fatigue. During peak competition block speed endurance will be completely phased out of the program.

At various times throughout the season, early progressions of certain training methods are implemented. For example, repeated 20m sprints are an effective method of stimulating an athlete 1-2 days prior to a competition to ensure sharpness is attained.

Strength & Power Development

The basics of how the strength program progresses throughout the year are discussed here. For greater detail of the strength training plan, see *Concepts of the Periodized Strength Training Program* later in this chapter.

Weight training is an important part of the training program. Most horizontal jumpers will spend 3-4 days per week in the weight room doing some kind of resistance training.

Each training phase has a different emphasis of strength training (for example, strength, maximal strength, power). However, all types of strength will be developed during each training phase in some quantity in order to continually improve all aspects of specific athletic performance.

During the **General Preparation Phase** overall intensity of weight training will naturally be lower than during the subsequent phases. During this time the athlete's fitness, strength and power will be at its lowest point and therefore the training load will reflect this.

It is important that during the early stages of preparation the athlete begins to increase resistance as soon as possible as this will begin to elicit specific adaptations to the CNS and muscular system.

The goal of strength development early in the training year is to prepare the body for the much heavier and more explosive work that will follow later in the program. The focus of exercise choice during this early period is to stimulate large muscle groups in as many ways as possible.

Exercises will be performed using a full range of motion mostly targeting the glutes, hamstrings and quadriceps. It is important during this time that exercise variety is large, as the greater the stimuli early-on, the larger the initial adaptation will be.

The need for specificity later on in the program makes it impossible to maintain a large variety in exercises throughout the year and therefore early variation is important.

Both the American and European-influenced training programs use a higher repetition scheme during this time. However, the American setup uses a lower repetition range and therefore does not target specific muscular hypertrophy like the European set-up does.

During the first **Specific Physical Conditioning Phase** the emphasis is on developing maximal strength and reactive strength and will therefore account for the majority of the weight training sessions. Exercise choice targets the prime movers mostly with a lower volume placed on developing upper-body strength.

During this phase the overall load for weight training is at its peak. Many sessions will include lifting very high percentages of the athlete's single-repetition max for 3-5 repetitions and therefore the sessions are very demanding.

Relaxation and recovery strategies between sessions are extremely important during this time.

Reactive strength development during this phase will consist of high intensity plyometrics and weighted jumping exercises. Constant monitoring of how the athlete is feeling is very important during this high-intensity 6-week training phase.

If, on a given day, the athlete is not feeling up to performing a certain session, it is vital to either rest completely or perform a much lighter version of the weight training session. Maximal strength and power training sessions should only be performed if the athlete is feeling well-rested and physically ready for the programmed session.

The **Technical or Special Preparation Phase** primarily targets maximal speed, approach development and specific preparation for full approach jumping.

The weight training during this phase is mainly for explosive power development. Exercise variety is limited during this phase as the key exercises for specific power development must be used and repeated over and over again with slight variations.

During this phase and throughout the Competition Phase maximal strength sessions will be performed only once every 1-3 weeks depending on the athlete and time of the year. These sessions are designed to maintain specific max strength and are therefore very short and target only prime muscle groups responsible for event-specific performance.

During the **Competition Phase** the most important aspect of training is to make sure the athlete is ready for competition that week. This means the training load needs to drop dramatically, with only 1-2 high intensity sessions performed the week of a competition.

This will enable a training effect known as *super-compensation* to occur. This is when the athlete is rested and his/her physical qualities that were depleted during hard training are now rejuvenated and at the level needed for optimum performance.

Power is the most important ability for all horizontal jumpers. It is the key determining factor for speed and force production and is therefore a priority over the course of the year. Power development occurs on Day One of the season and will remain a constant throughout each training phase.

During the early season, low intensity hopping and jumping movements are used to strengthen the tendons, ligaments and assistive muscles. These exercises teach correct foot contact action and muscle recruitment patterns that become more important as exercise intensity and specificity increases.

Jump capacity will also be developed using endurance bounding routines. These routines are sub-maximal in intensity and are used to develop leg stiffness, work capacity, technique and power endurance.

As the Competition Phase approaches, the quality of the power work increases. Much longer recovery periods are given, volume decreases, box height increases, time of ground contact decreases, and movement specificity increases.

For example, double leg plyometric work transition into single leg and standing bounding exercises transition into speed bounding with a running start.

As with almost all aspects of training, the athlete should start with broad general movements and exercises and shift toward a narrow range of specific movements that closely mimic the action, range of motion and force application of the specific event.

Listed below is a breakdown of how Strength/Power development, including plyometric exercises, are progressed and manipulated throughout the training year.

As previously discussed, each training block must have a different emphasis and overall load that changes throughout the year if ongoing physical development is going to occur.

Therefore, as with all other training elements, certain exercises and drills are more suitable for some training blocks than others. The correct timing of these exercises, and most importantly the progression of complexity, amplitude, direction, volume, and speed at which they are performed are essential for correct development.

These examples are similar throughout the American and European-influenced training setups.

Prime Weight Room Exercises and Plyometric Exercises General Progression Guide

General Prep	Specific Prep	Technical / Special Prep	Competition
Prime Weight Room Exercises			
Deep Squats Pause Squat Slow Squat Wide Squat	½ Squat ¼ Squat Eccentric Squat	¼ Squat Isometric Squat S/L Squat Jump Squat	¼ Squat Jump Squat Speed Squat S/L Reactive Squat
Dead lift Clean Pulls Power Clean	Power Clean Split Clean	Split Clean Hang Clean	Hang Split Clean Split Clean S/L Clean Catch
Deep Step up Slow Step up Walking Lunge Side Lunge	½ Step Up Standing Lunge	¼ Step up Reactive Step up Standing Lunge	Jump Step Up Reactive Step Up Reactive Lunge
Plyometric Exercises			
SLJ STJ Standing Bounds Endurance Bounds Power Skips Lin/Lat Hopping Stair Jumping Vertical Multi Jumps	4 Bounds & Jump 2 step up 4B&J Combination Bounds Hurdle Jumps Depth jumps (30cm) S/L Depth jumps (20cm) Power Skips	Speed Bounds 4-6 step 4B&J Hurdle hops Speed Combo Bounds Depth Jumps (60cm) S/L Depth jumps (40cm)	Speed Bounds Max 4B&J Hurdle hops + Sprint Depth Jump (90cm) S/L Depth Jumps (40cm)

Table 5

Technical Development

Technical development takes place 1-3 times per week depending on the athlete's technical level and time of the year. The main technical session is generally performed early in the week or after a rest day and consists of various full jumps from a short approach. For technical work most athletes will use a 10-14 stride run. This allows for enough speed and airtime to practice whole technique.

Many coaches use ramps or raised takeoff boards to practice flight technique with less effort for the takeoff. I have found this to do more harm than good. Although it does require less effort to achieve the needed height and airtime, it stresses the hip joints and glute muscles on one side to a degree that isn't recommended.

As the season progresses the number of running strides will also progress. Early on in the season the jumper may perform a high number of repetitions from a very short run (depending on skill level, 4-8 strides). This allows him/her to learn the correct movement and muscle firing patterns before adding greater speed to the takeoff action.

The secondary technical session of the week often includes *part technical* drills. These are various exercises that break down separate aspects of the jump. For example, the 1-2-3 drill focuses on the rhythm and timing of the final 3 strides and takeoff. There is a long list of drills that can be used during the secondary technical session.

The coach or athlete will determine which aspect of the jump needs to be broken down and practiced using the "part" method. It is very important to remember that "part technical" drills must be combined with "whole technical" drills if they are going to be of benefit. No drill or exercise can replace the need for practicing the entire skill at 90-100% + speed and effort.

After roughly 6-8 weeks of training, full approach work is added to the training program. The approach run is a hugely important technical aspect of the event and will require much repetition throughout the year.

The rhythm, stride pattern and accuracy component of the approach is something many jumpers find very difficult to master. This part of the event is something that often prevents very talented jumpers from competing at the top level or from remaining at the top level once they have achieved an elite distance.

I have seen many great jumpers who have never mastered the approach and therefore can never turn their great jumping ability into legal competition jumps.

Numerous approach-training strategies have been tried over the years, some with success and some without. Generally, however, there still remains an uncertainty over what is actually the best method for achieving accuracy and consistency with the approach.

The general approach styles include:

1. **The all-out approach** – Perform a maximal acceleration from the start.

2. **Gradual approach** – Perform a gradual acceleration from the start at a pre-determined pace and rhythm.

The all-out approach style is the least common among elite jumpers. It is, however, very common with youth jumpers. This style can create a couple of problems. Firstly, an aggressive start to the run often causes a rigid athlete who lacks the rhythm and elasticity needed and makes approach accuracy difficult to master.

Another issue relates to the conservation of explosive power. The long jump requires a single maximum effort takeoff and the ability to perform this is often affected when proceeded by a maximum effort acceleration. The triple-jump is slightly different. The second approach style is more common, but it too has various flaws.

Performing the same gradual acceleration again and again takes great practice and repetition. It is important to help maintain rhythm by placing markers on the track where specific foot strikes are supposed to hit. For example, the 12th step should hit at a certain point on the runway each time to maintain rhythm and accuracy.

This method enables relaxed sprinting and for optimal but not maximal speed to be achieved at the correct point on the runway. This method, however, proves difficult for younger inexperienced jumpers to master. It takes an athlete with great kinesthetic awareness to recreate the same acceleration pattern each and every time. Once mastered, however, it is likely the most successful approach method.

To help develop good spatial awareness and accuracy over the final 1-5 strides of the approach, I have conducted some research using a learning tool called *contextual interference* (CI). Essentially, this tool creates more difficulty while learning a skill within a practice setting. This in turn makes performing the skill easier in a competition setting because the skill will be in its most simple form (i.e., performing the normal task).

To make the CI high and thus make the practice of approach accuracy more difficult, the number of approach steps is changed in random order and/or the pre-determined approach start is moved back or forward.

These two strategies do not allow for consistency and therefore are always forcing the jumper to make adjustments in order to reach the board at speed. Over time the athlete will become better at dealing with a high CI effect and will find that during competition, when only one approach pattern is used, he/she will achieve accuracy much more easily. Below is a more detailed example of how Contextual Interference can be used throughout the season.

General Prep	• Build up to 3 variations of approach stride number during a session • Use consistent starting position for all jumps/approaches • Target short, long, and perfect aim of the board during sessions
Specific Prep / Technical Prep	1. • Build up to 3 variations of approach stride number during a session • Use consistent starting position for all jumps/approaches • Target short, long, and perfect aim of the board during sessions 2. • Vary starting method during jumps and approaches • Vary starting position by 30-60cm in alternating fashion • Keep board strike target constant, either short, long or perfect 3. • Use constant start position • Target specific points on board (2-8 inch specific)
Competition	• Short and full approach runs with a very specific focus point using constant starting position

Table 5.1

General Fitness Development

Although not a component of training that is greatly stressed, general fitness does help to get the athlete back into training again after the long recovery phase.

During the general preparation phase training includes various endurance circuits and slow tempo style running. The idea of the endurance circuits is to have the athlete perform various exercises with his/her heart rate remaining elevated for a long period of time.

Once specific training has started it is detrimental for development to continue building general fitness and endurance beyond the necessary level.

Speed endurance development and various types of exercises targeting injury prevention and general strength seem to maintain fitness levels well throughout specific and competition periods.

Concepts of the Periodized Strength Training Program

Flexible Undulating Weight Training Program (American Influence)

This particular weight training set-up has been largely influenced from American research and various practices. It is a successful method but one that I only recommend for very experienced coaches and athletes.

Weight training throughout the American influenced program is set up to be the second training session on that particular day. Here, the track workouts will always take precedent because they generally require more focus, coordination and energy.

Due to the order of the set-up, a flexible weight training program is often more beneficial. This is especially the case if the athlete is forced to perform the session after short rest from the track workout. The word "flexible" is used for good purpose. This kind of set-up is determined by the need of the athlete on a given day and not completely by a pre-determined program.

The flexible set-up allows the coach or athlete to perform the correct weight training session for that particular day depending on how the athlete is feeling.

This way a fatigued athlete will not feel obligated to battle his/her way through a maximal weight training session and instead will perform a medium or light weight training session which is aimed for recovery and general strength development.

It is particularly important that maximal strength and power training sessions are only performed when the athlete is at 90% or higher in terms of energy and performance capabilities. Assessment of the athlete's capabilities prior to a particular session can be performed various ways. Asking directly how the athlete is feeling prior to the workout can easily assess fatigue and motivation.

Physical capabilities can be quickly assessed after a warm-up by performing a vertical jump test, running vertical jump test, standing long jump or via power output from a jump squat if the gym is equipped with a power output computer device such as a Tendo Unit.

If the athlete is at 90% or greater of their best performance and they are mentally fresh, then they are able to perform a highly intense weight training session.

If the testing results are below 90%, an alternative easier weight training session should be performed. And if the test results are very low it may be best to cancel the session and rest instead.

The purpose of a flexible schedule like the one described above is to ensure that the athlete is performing as many high-quality training sessions as possible.

As previously mentioned, for speed/power athletes the quality of training performed far outweighs the importance of quantity. Each training session, no matter how light or intense, should be performed to the highest quality for the optimal training adaptations to occur.

Therefore, it is more beneficial for a fatigued athlete to perform a light weight training session that enhances recovery than to perform a power session when he/she is unable to produce bar speeds high enough to actually develop power.

This is a hard concept for most athletes to grasp because it is obvious that a power training session is more specific to performance gains than a light weight circuit. Therefore, most feel that performing a power session is always more beneficial regardless of the quality of the session. This is not the case and I cannot stress enough that during specific training phases (the majority of the year) training quality and mental and physical recovery is most important.

To ensure that the coach/athlete has options regarding which training session to perform prior to reaching the weight training facility, an "ideal" weight sequence for the phase is laid out.

For example, the Special Physical Conditioning Phase has a different ideal sequencing of particular weight training sessions than during the Technical Phase. During each phase there is a particular emphasis placed on specific weight training sessions (Medium loads, Maximum strength, Power).

Table 5.2 lists the types of weight training sessions performed over the course of the year during this set-up. The sessions target the development of different physical abilities. Guidelines for how to implement the different types of sessions are included.

Weight Training Type	Loading Guidelines (Reps & Weight %)	Focus
Very Light (VL)	Auxiliary Lifts – 15 – 20 reps Rehab Exercises – 10-20 reps	Recovery/Injury Rehabilitation
Light (L)	Auxiliary Lifts – 10-15 reps	General Strength/Recovery
Medium (M)	Olympic Lifts – 4-6 @80-85% Other prime Lifts – 6-8 @80-85%	Strength
Heavy (H)	Olympic Lifts – 3-5 @85-90% Other prime Lifts – 4-6 @85-90%	Strength/Max Strength
Very Heavy (VH)	Olympic Lifts – 1-2 @85+ % Other prime Lifts – 1-3 @90+ %	Maximum Strength/Explosive Power
Power (P)	Olympic Lifts – 1-4 @70-80% Other prime Lifts – 4-8 @30-50%	Power

Table 5.2

Table 5.3 below highlights the emphasis that should be given to the different weight training loads during the different phases of year. Understanding this becomes very important when using a flexible schedule with a fatigued athlete. To fully understand the sequencing options, see the American influenced training program in chapter 9.

Training Phase	Weight Training Emphasis	2 Week (6 session) Sequencing Plan
GPP	1. General Strength – L / M 2. Strength – H	L / M / H / M / L / H
SPC	1. Max Strength – H, VH 2. General / Strength – H, M, L 3. Power – P	H / M / VH / P / VH / M
Technical	1. Power – P 2. Strength – H 3. Max Strength – VH	P / H / P / VH / P / P
Competition	1. Power – P 2. Max Strength – VH, H 3. Strength – M 4. Recovery – L	VH / P / M / P / P / L

Table 5.3

All sessions are performed multiple times throughout a sequence and training phase, therefore when one session is missed due to fatigue or any other reason, the athlete simply continues with the normal sequence, not needing to make up the missed session.

However, if a power session is changed to a very light session and the next scheduled session is also very light, the athlete may want to perform a power session if he/she is in a specific training block.

The most important advice I can offer is this: Coaches, listen to your athletes; and athletes, listen to your bodies.

Linear Weight Training Program (European Influence)

The basic linear periodization method is commonly used and has been around for a long time. It undoubtedly works very well and is something I recommend for the majority of horizontal jumpers.

It is especially effective when used with slightly younger athletes and those who do not have an abundance of strength training history. It is important to note that elite jumpers and those with a long history of strength training will also benefit from this method. It is my preferred set-up for jumpers.

There are a few major differences between the Linear and Non Linear weight training set-up. The first major difference is the number of prime lifting sessions per week.

My linear (European Influenced) set-up requires 2 prime sessions per week instead of the 3 which the undulating set-up requires.

It is important to note, I am not speaking of the days that include *Weight Circuits* and *General Strength Circuits*. Although important, these supplementary strength sessions which aid recovery and the strengthening of assistive muscles are not classified as prime weight training sessions.

A prime session of any kind refers to one which develops specific performance capabilities and for a jumper is high-intensity by nature.

The European influenced system as a whole does not include any double prime session days. As a result the training is spread over 6 days with 1 day for complete rest.

This set-up allows each key training component (Speed/Power/Strength) to be given priority on a particular day. It also allows for a completely rested athlete to perform each session and aims to achieve the highest possible training quality.

The second major difference between weight training set-ups is the way the sessions are managed and progressed throughout the different phases of training. Each block or training phase in the European influenced program is designed around a certain element of strength development. These strength elements are listed in table 5.

The strength development from General Preparation through to the Competition Phase blends together seamlessly. Generally speaking, the number of repetitions starts high with lower weight and progresses to lower repetitions with high weight.

The addition of power development in the weight room is also blended in to coexist with maximum power development during the Technical or Special training block. During this block the addition of complex training can also be seen.

This method is useful for maintaining maximum strength while also developing explosive power. As with the American influenced system, during the Competition Phase the weight training volume is considerably decreased. Typically, 1 session shall be performed 3-4 days prior to the competition.

Table 5.4 below describes the purpose of the weight training program during each phase of training.

Training Phase	General Prep	Specific Prep	Technical/ Spec	Competition
Weight Training Goal	1. General Strength	1. Maximum Strength	1. Explosive Power 2. Maximum Strength	1. Explosive Power 2. Max Strength Maintenance

Table 5.4

The Horizontal Jumps

6

THE PERIODIZED TRAINING PROGRAM

Fully detailed breakdown of how the training program is put together into a complete plan. Includes charts, graphs and training plan samples.

Nick Newman
The Horizontal Jumps: Plannin
for Long Term Development

CHAPTER 6

THE PERIODIZED TRAINING PROGRAMS

The previous chapters have covered almost every aspect of training needed to be a successful horizontal jumper. First, I discussed important technical aspects of the horizontal jumps. I placed the Technical chapter ahead of all training chapters as it is extremely important that all athletes have a solid foundation of technical training before performing an advanced training program. I then introduced which physical abilities are important for long and triple jumping from a training perspective. I also detailed various training methods that are successfully used for developing those specific physical abilities.

Chapter 5 went a step further and described how those training methods are planned and periodized during the long track and field season. For the information within the previous chapters to fully make sense and be used successfully, it is essential that the coach or athlete understand the relationship of each training component and how they interact with one another. The periodized training program does exactly that. It describes the careful planning of the daily, weekly, and monthly training and how all of the individual components are combined and manipulated to ensure development occurs throughout the season.

CONCEPTS OF THE PERIODIZED TRAINING PROGRAM

The yearly training program follows many general guidelines from which each important ingredient is carefully manipulated and progressed over time. By definition, the program is undulating (non linear) in design although the individual components of the program progress in a linear fashion during each individual training phase. I believe this is similar for most successful programs when analyzed closely. The reason for the undulating model is because for a jumper to reach peak performance, many specific fitness components need to be at an optimal level at the same time. Another key reason is that many non-specific abilities play a major role in the continued development of the specific ones. Addressing all needs for a horizontal jumper are difficult to manage when long periods of training pass without placing the necessary attention on developing the specific bio-motors.

A successful training program is essentially the combination of various training phases performed and repeated multiple times throughout the year in many different ways giving the body the opportunity to continually adapt.

To ensure the ongoing development of the athlete, it is vital that three important training variables are manipulated throughout the year. These variables are intensity, volume, and specificity. The manipulation of these variables needs to occur smoothly and in a systematic manner. The changes of each training variable over the year would look like a wave pattern if graphed. The variable would have a slightly different wave pattern. The wave symbolizes how the variable is increased and decreased during various times of the year.

The most important variables determining the training load of each day, week, phase, and year are volume and intensity. The training load is the combination of both variables and is often written as (*Volume x Intensity*). The manipulation of training load is the single most important aspect of the periodized training program. Volume is the quantity of overall work performed within a session, week or training phase. It includes aspects of training such as amount of repetitions and sets, the number of exercises used, and the amount of training sessions performed.

The amount of total lifts, ground contracts, sprints, jumps, and any other training performed must be recorded to aid the planning of subsequent training. Volume is an easily abused aspect of training, especially with younger athletes. It is important to understand the relationship between volume and several factors.

Firstly, an athlete with less training experience will adapt quickly from lower volumes of specific training. Depending on the athlete's genetic ability they may even develop to a high level from low training volumes. An athlete with many years of specific training experience who is already at a high level would likely be the opposite. They would need and be able to tolerate higher training volumes. In order to continually reach higher levels of performance, volume will need to increase slowly over time. Is it important to note that not all training components may need to increase in volume.

As previously mentioned, athletes will vary in different athletic abilities. For one athlete, gradually increasing speed training volume may result in greater jumping distance. For another, a gradual increase in strength training volume may be needed. The increase in volume of one training component will affect the overall load of the program so I stress a careful approach to volume manipulation.

I generally advise introducing training volume at the cautiously low end for most athletes. Volume should reach the peak toward the end of pre-season training and drop as the competitive season approaches. Monitoring such things as test results throughout pre-season, motivation levels, and sleep patterns will give the coach and athlete a good indication if training volume is at the optimal level.

Training intensity is also very important and is an ultra-specific variable for a horizontal jumper because of the nature of the event. Intensity and volume are very closely related and the planning of one will not happen without the planning of the other. Intensity can be determined by several factors. In strength training it is easily quantified as the amount of weight being used relative to the athlete's one-repetition max, but it should not be forgotten that effort and bar speed also contribute to intensity.

Horizontal jumpers perform a large part of their training away from the weight room. Speed of movement relative to one's fastest speed is another important way to measure intensity and is used during all sprinting sessions. For plyometric training, intensity can be measured by height of the box during a depth jump, the run-in speed of bounding exercises and the effort employed during each jump. Training intensity for a horizontal jumper will be predominantly high throughout the entire season. This is because in order for specific adaptations to occur the athlete must train in a specific way.

The jumps are an explosive, maximum effort, high velocity, and high speed coordinative discipline and therefore specific training will have the same characteristics. However, throughout pre-season training it is important that intensity is able to increase slightly. As the athlete increases his/her performance levels and as training specificity reaches the highest point, it will become increasingly important for development that training intensity matches the level needed for competition performance. The wave pattern for intensity is slightly different than for volume and will reach the peak as the peak competition approaches.

Training specificity is a slightly different progression from the previous variables and is a very linear progression: overall training specificity with increase throughout pre-season leading the competition block. Everything we do in the training program is working toward the end goal of increasing jump performance. So in a sense everything in the program can be described as specific. However, there is a specificity continuum which should be used, and in general terms training starts at the low end and finishes at the high end of specificity. I feel this aspect of training planning is easily and often abused.

Specificity of training is an important factor when preventing early peaking or mental and physical fatigue. Therefore, it is very important that General Preparation is exactly that. Adaptations to specific training can happen very fast, especially for young athletes.

Therefore, prolonging the use of all specific training methods can have great effects on long term development. Higher-level, more experienced athletes will need more specific early training to achieve the same adaptations. General training is very beneficial for all athletes. In general it is recommended to gradually increase the use of specific training throughout the training phases and decrease the use of non-specific training.

For example, if we look at the progression of speed development during my American Influenced and European Influenced training blocks, you will see that the General Preparation Phase includes considerably less speed development than the Specific training blocks.

As previously discussed, non-specific training is essential and should not be overlooked as it is needed for developing and maintaining general fitness, bone and ligament strength, and overall injury prevention. It also plays an important restoration role for the central nervous system and breaks up the monotony and mental bashing of high-intensity training. During the European Influenced training set-up general circuit training, extensive tempo work serves as important recovery time for the CNS as well as strength development for auxiliary muscle groups and general fitness development.

As intensity and training specificity increase, training volume decreases. High levels of all three variables will co-exist for a very short time just before training volume begins to decrease.

TRAINING LOAD DISTRIBUTION

The distribution of load throughout each week, phase and training year largely determines the development success of the athlete. The inclusion of all training components and the manipulation of the training variables combine to produce the periodized training plan.

There are many methods for distributing training loads. Each method is slightly unique but in general they all achieve the same outcome. The basic purpose behind each is to overload, recover, and overload again. This cycle is essential as constant overload will cause overtraining and constant recovery will cause detraining. For the body to maintain a steady development it must be shocked or stressed by training, allowed to recover and grow, and then get shocked again. Each time the athlete is allowed to recover from a training session his or her ability will slightly improve. The repetition of this cycle for a long enough period of time will improve the specific athletic ability being targeted. The recovery process and loading differs greatly between the two methods detailed in this book.

The American influenced system places a large emphasis on the training during 3 main days per week (Mon/Wed/Fri) and therefore has specific days planned for recovery purposes. USA option B program uses 4 high load training days (Sun/Mon/Wed/Thurs) and also uses specific days designed around recovery purposes. The European system differs in that the training load is distributed over 6 days in more of an equal fashion. This enables several back-to-back high intensity days with the afternoon and night serving as recovery.

During both the American and European influenced training programs I prescribe a basic step loading pattern for the load distribution throughout each training phase of the year. Except for the General Preparation Phase (GPP), the step loading method is called *reverse step loading*. Any step loading method uses loading variations over of a day, week and/or entire cycle of training. These variations are essential for ensuring that training changes in intensity and volume in a way that promotes ongoing adaptation and performance improvement.

The General Preparation Phase uses a normal or forward step loading pattern. This means that over the course of the 4 week cycle the training load will increase each week for the first 3 weeks and then dramatically decrease during the 4th and final week which acts as the regeneration week. Using the normal step loading pattern during the first cycle is important for a number of reasons.

Firstly, General Preparation is usually performed following a lengthy rest period in which a certain amount of detraining will occur. Normal step loading will therefore allow the athlete to slowly work his way back into training during this time. Adaptation will occur fairly fast after a long rest period and therefore the first 3 weeks will progress accordingly. As the ability to again handle the demands of consistent training returns the athlete will be ready to return to more specific training.

As specificity increases throughout the training blocks following General Preparation, so does the need for quality training. Quality is the key reason I introduce a reverse step loading method for the remainder of the season. This method is simply a reverse of normal step loading and allows the hardest training week (highest load) to be performed after the previous regeneration or unloading week. As the athlete naturally fatigues from the hard week the training load becomes lighter. This allows for greater physical and psychological super-compensation to occur. In my experience, 3-week reverse step loading cycles produce improvements in all specific bio-motor abilities consistently throughout the season and reduce the number of "flat" feeling days during training.

Training phases are shortened from 4 weeks to 3 weeks because shorter specific training phases promote greater adaptation over a long period. It also allows more frequent evaluation and unloading during high intensity training. The psychological aspect of this loading system should also not be overlooked. An athlete experiencing burnout from constantly increasing training loads cannot maintain high training quality for very long.

THE WEEKLY PLAN

With the loading plan for the season in place and the competition schedule somewhat set, we can now begin to establish how the weekly training plan will look. Although many factors need to be accounted for when designing the weekly plan, it is most important that the end goals for the season are in place. The weekly loading patterns differ substantially based on which program set-up you follow and they are described later in this chapter.

The most important reason for the specific layout of the weekly training is to ensure the overload/recovery cycle can occur. There are many ways to successfully arrange a weekly set-up. The two set-ups I recommend work specifically within the training plan for whom they were written. Therefore you should not mismatch training and training set-ups from the two programs offered in this chapter.

AMERICAN INFLUENCED WEEKLY PLAN

The American influenced training program follows the notion that hard training days are followed by easy or medium training days. A hard day of training for a horizontal jumper will generally consist of variations of sprinting, plyometrics and weight training exercises. These double training session days are highly fatiguing for the central nervous system and recovery generally takes up to 48 hours.

Therefore, these training sessions are purposely scheduled 48 hours apart. As previously stated, "easy" days follow each hard CNS training session. In this context an easy day is far less stressful for the CNS and therefore acts as a recovery day for that system. An easy day, however, may not be all that easy for the athlete. For example, this day could include weight circuits, tempo running or specific technical work performed at a lower intensity. The easy days can be extremely valuable for the athlete by providing time to aid the recovery process. The layout of training for this set-up follows a Medium/ High/ Low/ Medium/ High/ Low routine over a 6 day training week.

With this set-up the athlete performs jump specific training days after each easy/recovery day for optimal performance during the most specific session of the week. Technical days require the most skilled performances and therefore require a fresh and rested athlete. Strength training sessions which have an eccentric strength focus will also be scheduled during the early part of the week as they are very demanding on the athlete. The double speed/weights training day is followed by a recovery day due to the taxing nature of the session.

The USA Influence option B program groups the training components slightly differently but still issues multiple days per week for recovery. During this set-up jump specific technical training is prescribed prior to but on the same day as weight training. Speed development sessions are placed prior to but on the same day as plyometric training. This set-up is an extremely effective way of programming but should be saved for an advanced athlete with a longer training history. The first USA Influence program discussed would be a good starting point before incorporating a method using back-to-back double training days such as Option B.

EUROPEAN INFLUENCED WEEKLY PLAN

The loading for this set-up is dispersed over a 6 day week. There is one moderate to high load training session along with a light secondary session per day. This set-up is based around the theory that CNS recovery from a single high intensity session takes around 24 hours. Ideally each main training session is performed in the morning after a full night of sleep. The afternoon and evening of each day will focus on the recovery of the CNS in some form using the specific recovery methods discussed in Chapter 4.

Although there are several different options regarding the layout of the weekly training, I recommend a simple layout of Jumps/ Sprints/ Weights/ Jumps/ Sprints/ Weights/ REST as the 7 day plan. With this set-up the second Jumps days is generally the lowest load day of the 6 day training cycle. The highest load jump day with longer approach technical work and high intense plyometrics will be performed after the only REST day of the week. Speed sessions which require high speed complex coordination and high CNS stress will follow the lowest load days of the week. Weight training sessions are placed last in each 3 day mini-cycle as they are of least importance relative to technical and speed development. If a particular session is substituted with a recovery session or lost in any way it is recommended the athlete simply continue with the regular cycle of the week whenever ready.

INDIVIDUAL TRAINING PHASES

Once the loading parameters for the season are set, the coach or athlete can begin to input training methods and individual exercises into each phase. During the previous chapters many of these exercises and training protocols have been discussed. An effective program implements each training method strategically based on the primary and secondary goals of the training phase. Perhaps the most important principle to adhere to is that of progression. Each training phase needs to blend into one another seamlessly and be a natural progression of the phase before.

The four main training phases throughout the year are General Preparation, Specific Preparation, Special or Technical Preparation and Competition Phase. The purpose of having such phases is to help organize training components into smaller more manageable time frames. The names of the different phases are unimportant and depending upon whom you talk to can take on many versions. It is the purpose and goal of each phase to make them unique and extremely important to the development of the athlete. Each goal of the training phases must build on one another and work toward achieving the end goal of the year.

More often than not the end goal is to jump farther than before and to do it at a specific time in the competition calendar. Therefore, all goals must be related and should be specific to the end goal and needs of the athlete.

Remember, the majority of the training year is to be spent performing specific training. The progression of training throughout the phases should therefore be athlete and event specific.

It is also important to remember that the terms "general" and "specific training" are relative. For example, long slow running is not building a general base for acceleration development. Always remember what it is you are actually trying to build a base for.

A horizontal jumper needs to be fast, strong, powerful, and highly coordinated and therefore all training should be related to these goals in some way.

General Preparation Phase

General Preparation or *GPP* is usually the first training phase performed by the athlete after an off-season break. It is common for an athlete to have rested or actively rested for 4-6 weeks leading up to the start of the new season.

Therefore the GPP is designed to progressively return the athlete back to the rigors of high intensity training. Some say this first phase is training the athlete to train again. This is somewhat true. However, it must prepare the athlete for the type of training he/she will be performing and not just for general training. Where many coaches make a mistake is in thinking that no matter the event the GPP is the same for all. At the very least, speed/power athletes should be grouped together for general training which is far different than the general training for the mid distance athletes.

As seen in the breakdown listed below, General Preparation involves nearly all training components similar to the specific phases. However, during this early phase these components are developed using the least specific methods. For example, a long jump takeoff may still be included in training but it may be performed slowly at low intensity in sneakers while jumping over multiple low hurdles placed on a grass field.

The most specific method for including a long jump takeoff into training would be from full speed off a takeoff board into the pit. The development of acceleration using the least specific methods also begins during GPP. For example, repeating very short sprints from various starting positions is a common method used for developing start mechanics and an explosive initial impulse. These may also be performed in sneakers and/or on a grass field.

The most specific method of developing acceleration would be from an upright stance on a track in spikes over 30-40m distance. Every component of training can be manipulated and changed using many progressions throughout the training year. As long as your progressions used throughout GPP develop the abilities needed during the subsequent phases of training, the desired training effect should occur. It is important to include a lot of training stimulus during early stages of training.

Variety of exercises/drills can be very high as specificity is relatively low. The progression of intensity is also an important factor during early training. The aim is to gradually increase intensity and volume (training load) throughout the early phase as the athlete becomes comfortable handling the new training load.

The General Preparation Phase aims to achieve the following:

- Improved anaerobic fitness
- Improved general fitness
- Improved starting and acceleration mechanics
- General total body strength
- Flexibility, Mobility and Coordination

Below is a detailed breakdown of what is to be included in the General Preparation phase:

- Acceleration development (10-30m)
    - Various starts
    - Med ball throw into sprints
- Elasticity development
    - Multi Jump circuits
    - Low intense hopping/bounding
    - Agility drills
- General Strength
    - 6-10 repetition weight training
    - Large muscle groups
    - Slow/Medium rep speed
- General Fitness
    - Endurance circuits
    - Core fitness/stability
    - Tempo/Form running
    - General strength circuits
    - Flexibility work

The Horizontal Jumps

DAILY LOADING CHART DURING GENERAL PREPARATION PHASE – USA INFLUENCE

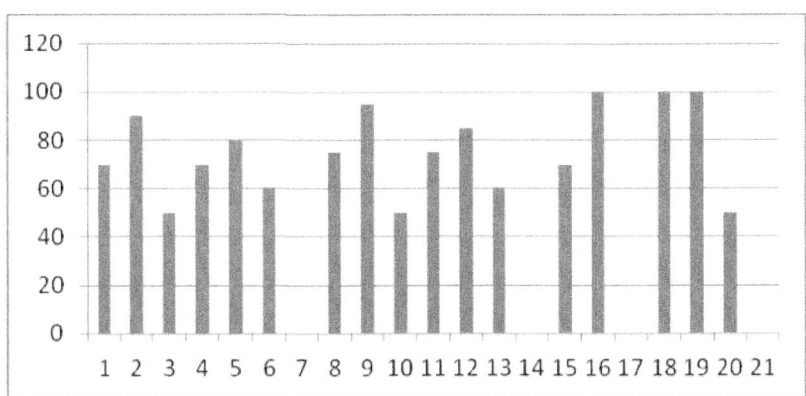

Graph 6: Daily Loading Plan for a 3 week GPP. The Daily Loading Plan varies from week to week, here shown for Week 1-3.

The graph above illustrates the loading set-up during a 4 week General Preparation Phase using the USA Influenced program.

The graph below illustrates the loading set-up during a 4 week General Preparation Phase using the USA Influenced program.

DAILY LOADING CHART DURING GENERAL PREPARATION PHASE – EUROPEAN INFLUENCE

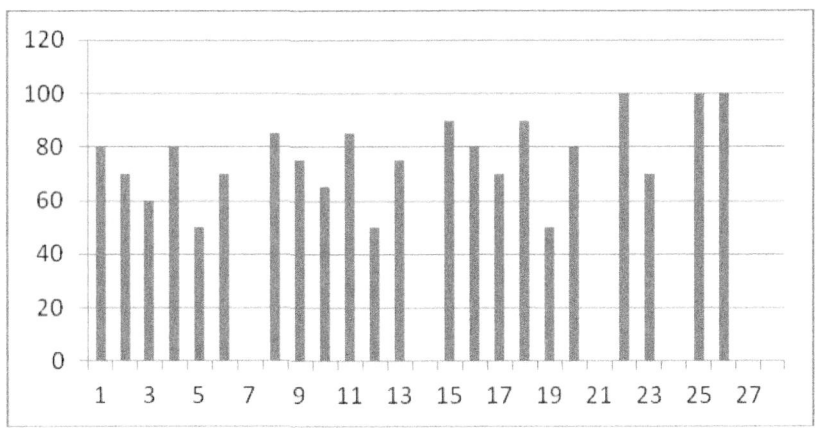

Graph 6.1: Daily Loading Plan for a 4 week GPP. The Daily Loading Plan varies from week to week, here shown for Weeks 1-4.

Specific Physical Conditioning

After a 4-8 week GPP the body has been reintroduced to full time training again. During the first specific training block athletes will begin to run faster, jump farther and lift heavier on a regular basis. Just as the General Preparation phase laid the ground work for the following phase, Specific Physical Conditioning or *SPC* will also lay the ground work for training performed during the most specific training called the *Special* or *Technical training phase*.

The goal of SPC is to prepare the athlete to become as fast and as powerful as possible to get ready for the Competition Phase. Achieving this is a step by step process which starts from day one of the GPP. It is during SPC however that much of the specific training will start.

As discussed in earlier chapters, the primary factor contributing to speed and power is maximum force production. Therefore maximum strength training becomes a priority during the first specific training phase. Almost all training goals of SPC are related to developing maximum strength. Starting and acceleration speed, for example, are also priorities during SPC, as they will become essential for the development of maximum speed during Special or Technical training later on. Jumping strength is another important focus during SPC and the inclusion of weighted plyometric exercises will increase training intensity considerably.

Performing relatively fast reactive movements against resistance serves as a great foundation for the maximum speed reactive training of the Special or Technical phase. Event specific technical training will begin during SPC also. Over the course of specific training the athlete will perform many short approach takeoffs into the pit. Technical focus must be a priority for most of the year and will transition from part focus to whole focus. Part technical training includes breaking down individual aspects of the jump and drilling it over and over again.

For example, a drill may simply emphasize the free leg swinging action in isolation. Part technical training can be useful for reminding certain technical cues but must be performed alongside full jumps from short approaches. Whole technical training includes the full action being performed and should be the focus for advanced jumpers. Generally over the course of specific training the technical training will gradually increase in specificity and intensity. Short approach jumps will increase running strides and as result takeoff speed and jump distance should increase.

The Specific Physical Conditioning Phase aims to achieve the following:

- Maximum Strength
- Acceleration Speed
- Elastic/Reactive Power
- Part to whole technical development
- Approach rhythm development
- Low end static power

Below is a more detailed breakdown of what is to be included in the Specific Physical Conditioning Phase:

- Long acceleration development 30-60m (2x week)
- Explosive power development (3x week)
    - Weighted jumping exercises
    - Weighted long jumps
    - Sled pull sprints
- Reactive power development (3x week)
    - BW jumping exercises
    - BW bounding variations
    - BW box jumps
- Strength development
    - Max strength (2x week)
    - Explosive strength (1x week)
    - General strength (1-2x week)
- Technical development (1x week)
    - 8-12 stride long/triple jumps
    - Full approaches away from the runway
- Tempo/Endurance maintenance (1x week)
    - Rhythm runs over 100-200m

Special/Technical Preparation

At this point the athlete is strong and explosive at slower speeds. He/she has probably produced some very promising short approach jump distances and is expecting big things from the upcoming season. The Special Preparation phase will play an essential role in converting the athlete's ability to produce maximum force into the ability to produce maximum **HIGH SPEED** force. Without the development of high speed force or rate of force development (RFD) the difference between short and full approach distance will be small and not as expected. In my opinion it is the Special Preparation phases that the majority of coaches miscalculate and yet they are the most important phases of the year.

The 10-12 weeks of training leading up to Special Preparation develop the abilities needed for optimal maximum speed and power development to be able to occur. As the two most important factors in determining jump distance, speed and power become center stage leading up to the competition season. During Special Preparation the majority of training is performed at high speed, maximum intensity, and with the highest technical proficiency possible. Weight room training becomes highly specific with many exercises focusing on unilateral (single leg) movements performed at maximum speed. The reduction in maximum strength work and thus in the use of heavy slow lifting will have a significant affect on muscular contraction speeds and high speed coordination and will transfer to greater sprinting speeds almost instantly. The intensity of track workouts during this phase will be at the highest point as a result. Plyometric training will also reach maximum intensity during this phase. Bounding will be performed at high running speeds for maximum distance and depth jumping will be from the highest boxes. Event specific technical work will also be performed at greater speeds and from longer approach distances. Maximum strength training will need to be performed once every 1-2 weeks for maintenance purposes.

Needless to say the adaptations resulting from a successful Special Preparation phase can be huge. However, this does not come without high risk and it is this phase that has the highest potential for injury. The quality of training must be stressed beyond anything else during this phase. Fatigued athletes should reduce the volume of high intensity exercises within a workout or perform a recovery style session instead. Longer than usual rest periods are especially common during this phase as maximum speed or power cannot be achieved under fatigued conditions. Performing recovery techniques between workouts and continuing with general strength/injury prevention training will help ensure the athlete remains injury free.

The Special/Technical Preparation Phase aims to achieve the following:

- Maximum sprinting speed
- Rate of Force Development
- Explosive Power
- High speed whole technical development
- Approach rehearsal and steering development
- Maximum Strength maintenance

Below is a more detailed breakdown of what is to be included in the Technical Phase:

- Maximum speed development (2x week)
    - Approaches
    - Fly sprints
    - SFS (60-120m)
    - Speed end runs
- Acceleration development (1-2x week)
    - 20-40m
- Technical development (2x weeks)
    - 12-16 stride long jumps
    - Full approach long jumps
- Explosive/Reactive power development (2x week)
    - Box jumps
    - Bounding
- Strength development
    - Max strength (1x week)
    - Explosive strength (2x week)
    - General strength (1-2x week)

The graph below illustrates the loading set-up for a 6 week SPC or Special Preparation phase using USA influence program option A.

DAILY LOADING CHART FOR THE SPECIFIC PHYSICAL CONDITIONING & TECHNICAL PHASE

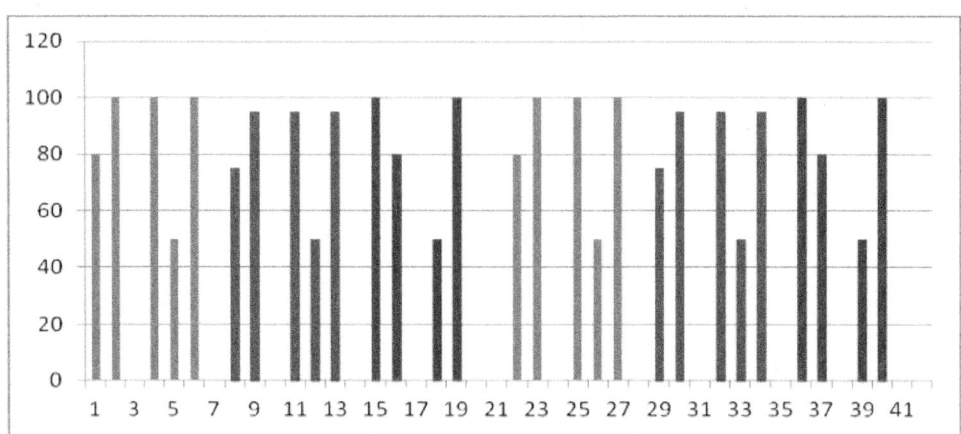

Graph 6.2: Daily Loading Plan for SPC & Technical phase. The Daily Loading Plan varies from week to week.

The graph below illustrates the loading set-up for a 6 week SPC or Special Preparation phase using USA influence program option B.

DAILY LOADING CHART FOR THE SPECIFIC PHYSICAL CONDITIONING & TECHNICAL PHASE – USA OPTION B

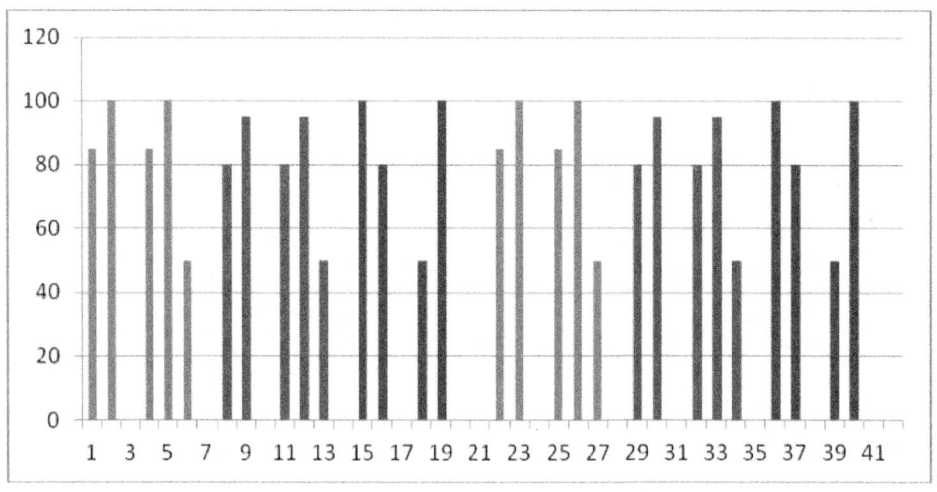

Graph 6.3: Daily Loading Plan for SPC & Technical phase. The Daily Loading Plan varies from week to week.

The graph below illustrates the loading set-up for a 6 week SPC or Special Preparation phase using the European Influenced program.

DAILY LOADING CHART FOR THE SPECIFIC PHYSICAL CONDITIONING & TECHNICAL PHASE – EUROPEAN INFLUENCE

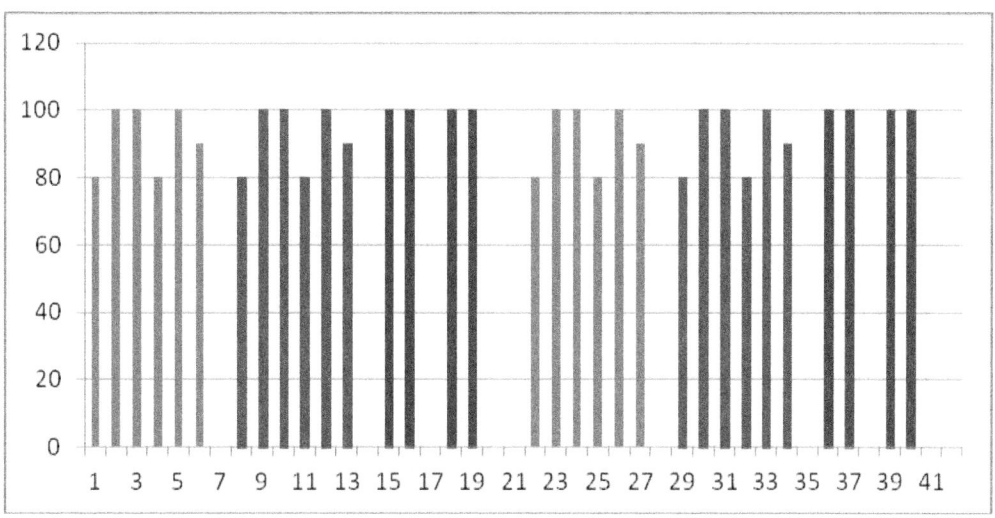

Graph 6.4: Daily Loading Plan for SPC & Technical phase. The Daily Loading Plan varies from week to week.

Competition Phase

The Competition Phase will see a considerable drop in overall training volume. As a result the accumulation of training from the previous months will bring forth some noticeable performance gains. Throughout the Competition Phase athletes should feel very light, fast, explosive, and effortless during nearly all workout sessions. Training intensity is kept high throughout but with extra rest days the athletes will be mentally and physically ready to compete at their highest level. During competition periods of longer than 2 weeks, maximum strength training including power cleans, squats and step-ups should be performed every 10-14 days.

The maintenance of maximum strength is of extra importance during long periods of training with decreased volume. It is also important to understand the relationship between early, main and peak competitions with the set-up of the competition week. Early season competitions of little importance will require minimal change from the regular weekly training schedule. A single day 1-2 days prior to the competition will be scheduled for recovery purposes. Main season and peak competition weeks require an extra focus on recovery and will be set-up differently than other weeks. One to two mid week recovery sessions along with a pre-competition recovery session will be scheduled.

The Competition Phase aims to achieve the following:

- Rest and recovery
- Maximum sprinting speed
- Approach rehearsal and steering development
- Rate of Force Development
- Explosive Power Development
- Maximum Strength maintenance

Below is a more detailed breakdown of what is to be included in the Competition Phase:

- Maximum speed development (1x week)
- Acceleration development (1x week)
- Explosive strength development (1-2 week)
- Explosive/reaction power development (1x week)
- Technical development (1x week)

The graph below illustrates the loading set-up for an early season Competition Phase using USA influence program.

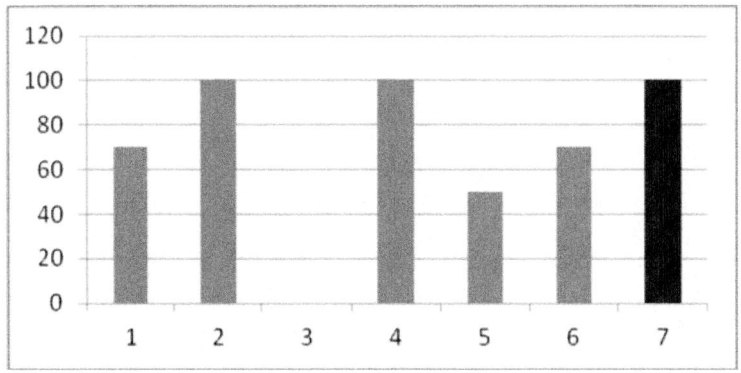

Graph 6.5: Daily Loading Plan for an early season competition week. Here the competition is shown in black and is preceded by a medium load day.

The 6.6 below illustrates the loading set-up for a main season Competition Phase using USA influence program:

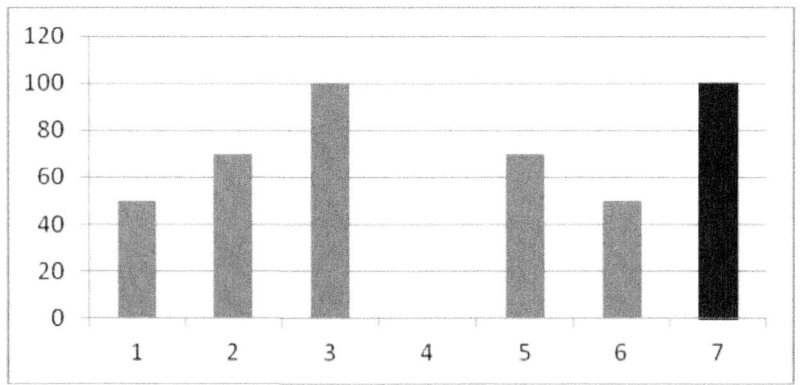

Graph 6.6: Daily Loading Plan for a main season competition week. Here the competition is shown in black and is preceded by a low load day.

The graph below illustrates the loading set-up for a peak season Competition Phase using USA influence program.

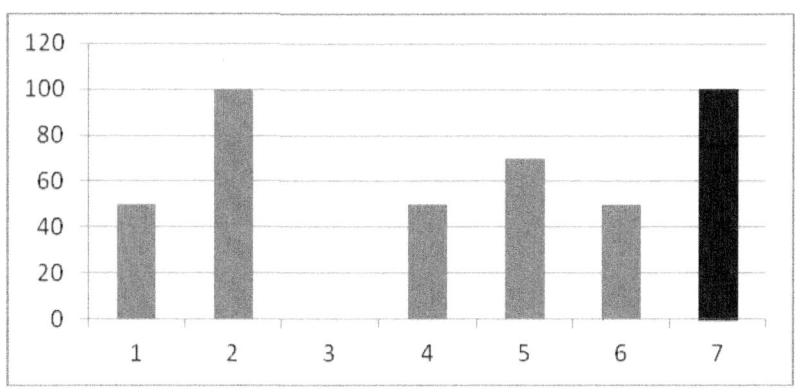

Graph 6.7: Daily Loading Plan for a main season competition week. Here the competition is shown in black and is preceded by a several medium or low load days.

The graph below illustrates the loading set-up for an early season Competition Phase using the European influence program.

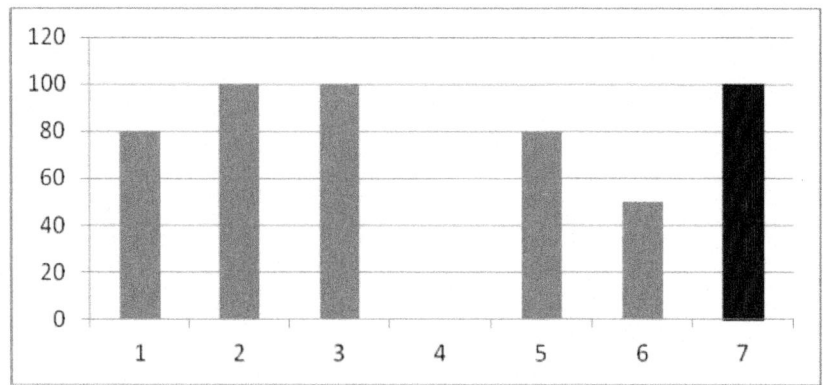

Graph 6.8: Daily Loading Plan for an early season competition week. Here the competition is shown in black and is preceded by a low load day.

The graph below illustrates the loading set-up for a main season Competition Phase using the European influence program.

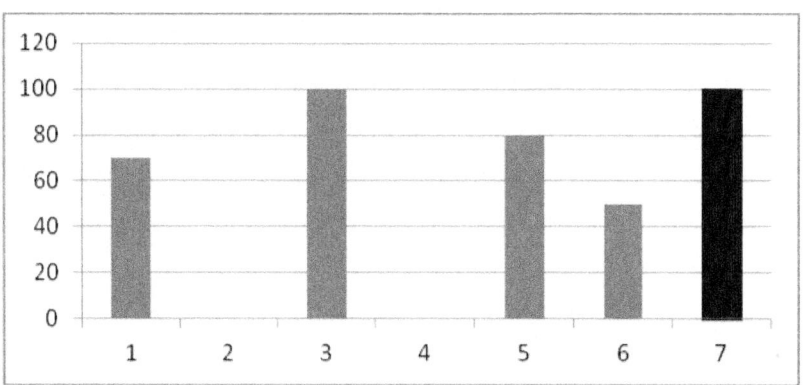

Graph 6.9: Daily Loading Plan for a main season competition week. Here the competition is shown in black and is preceded by a medium and low load day.

The graph below illustrates the loading set-up for a peak season Competition Phase using USA influence program.

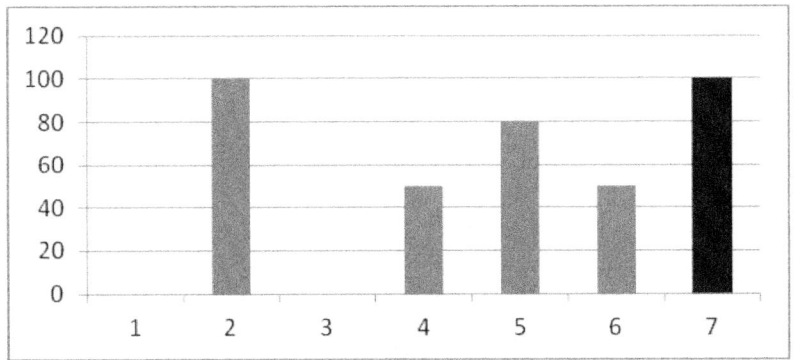

Graph 6.9: Daily Loading Plan for a main season competition week. Here the competition is shown in black and is preceded by a several medium or low load days.

COMBINING THE TRAINING PHASES

How the training phases will fit into the yearly plan will change based on how the competition schedule is to be performed. Typically, a single periodized set-up focusing solely on the outdoor season or a double periodized set-up including both indoor and outdoor season will be used.

Below are the recommended phase lengths depending on the type of periodization set-up you are using. Please note that it is perfectly acceptable to repeat training blocks multiple times during a season. SPC 1, 2, and 3, for example, could all be very similar in content and continue to produce the desired training adaptations. The athlete or coach will be able to determine whether or not a phase or which elements of a particular phase were successful and would be worth repeating.

SINGLE PERIODIZED SEASON

- **GPP** – 8 weeks
- **SPC 1** – 6 weeks
- **Special/Technical 1** – 6 weeks
- **SPC 2** – 3 weeks
- **Special/Technical 2** – 6 weeks

- **Competition 1** – 2-4 weeks
- **SPC 3** – 3 weeks
- **Special/Technical 3** – 3 weeks
- **Competition 2** – 6-8 weeks
- **REST** – 4-6 weeks

DOUBLE PERIODIZED SEASON

- **GPP** – 4 weeks
- **SPC 1** – 6 weeks
- **Special/Technical 1** – 6 weeks
- **Competition 1** – 4-6 weeks
- **REST** – 1 week
- **SPC 2** – 6 weeks
- **Special/Technical** – 6 weeks
- **Competition 2** – 2 weeks
- **SPC 3** – 3 weeks
- **Special/Technical 3** – 3 weeks
- **Competition 3** – 4-6 weeks
- **REST** – 4 weeks

The graphs below are examples of how the loading distribution and phase arrangement could occur throughout the season. Each shade on the graph signifies a different training phase and black are competition weeks. You will notice the reverse loading pattern occurring after the initial General Preparation Phase (RED) has completed. You will also see each third week after the initial phase is at 50% load. This is the regeneration week and is the same for competition weeks also. As with both a single periodized (Outdoor season) and double periodized (Indoor & Outdoor season) training blocks emphasizing the same physical abilities are repeated multiple times.

The Horizontal Jumps

LOADING CHART FOR FULL OUTDOOR SEASON

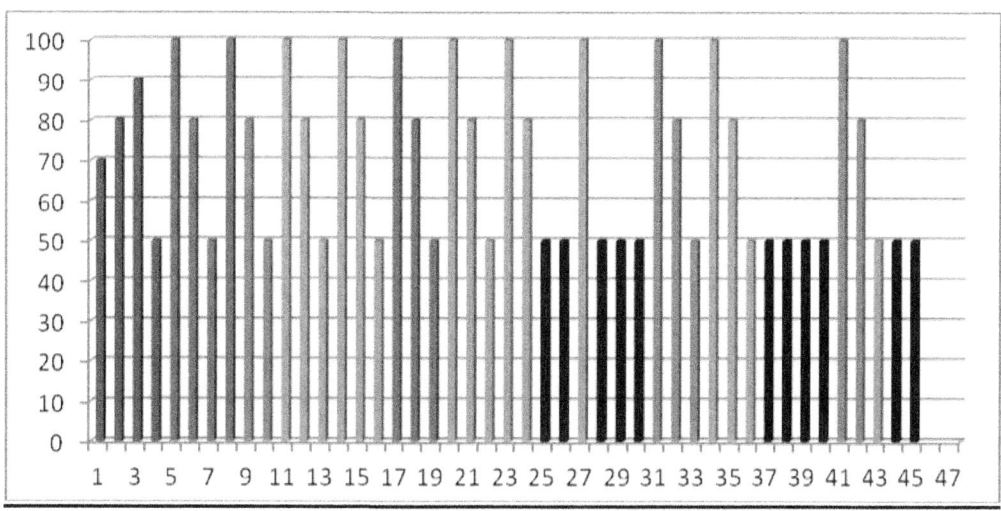

Graph 7: Loading Chart for a single peak outdoor Season. The season is broken into multiple phases including, General Preparatory, Specific Physical Conditioning, Technical, and Competition.

LOADING CHART FOR FULL INDOOR/OUTDOOR SEASON

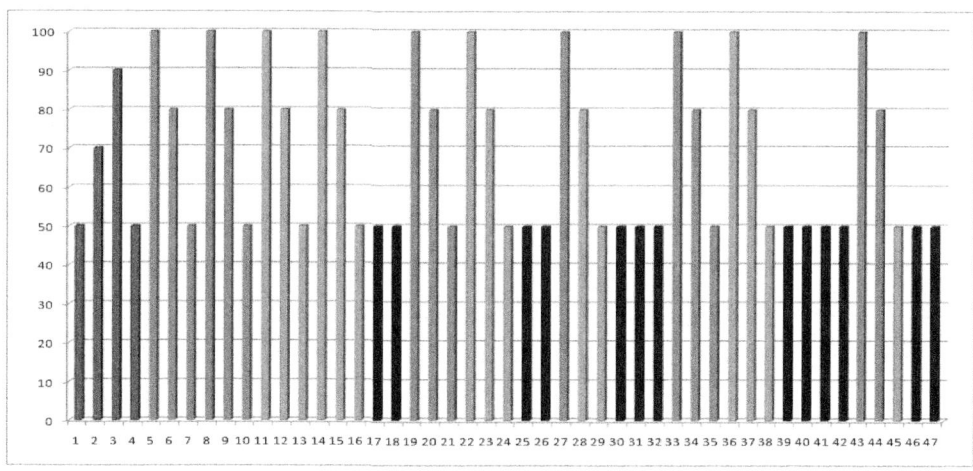

Graph 7.1: Loading Chart for a Double peak Indoor/Outdoor Season

TAPERING/PEAKING

Achieving a desired performed at a particular time or specific competition is what coaches and athletes continually strive for. This concept is known as a taper. When preparing for competitions the training load drops considerably and as a result the athlete's ability to perform is maximized. The specific details and percentage load decrease needed to achieve the taper will be based off training performed from the SPP through to the peak of the season. The reduction of training-induced fatigue on the psychological and physiological state can be profound. The athlete will experience significant physical gains resulting in increased confidence and motivation leading into competition time. Although the idea of a taper is very simple, implementing a successful taper can be somewhat complex and making mistakes can be very easy.

Considerations for a Taper

There are several ways to reduce training loading when trying to achieve a competition taper. Manipulations to intensity, volume, frequency, recovery, and training set-up are important ways of reducing overall load. However, it is also important to consider the length of the Competition Phase and the resulting taper and the type of taper used. The coach/athlete must understand how all factors relate and contribute toward achieving a successful taper.

Training Intensity

For a horizontal jumper it is recommended that training intensity alter very little during a taper. Maintaining high intensity training (90-100%) will achieve event specific adaptations and help maintain previously induced realized training adaptations.

Training Volume

Reducing volume is the most commonly used method for achieving a taper. It is common to see a reduction of 50-70% of total training volume during a taper period. The exact percentage decrease depends on previous training loads and whether the taper is going to be a progressive or non-progressive taper. In line with the programming, I suggest in this book a progressive taper is likely to be used. Therefore a gradual reduction in training volume is recommended. In this method a reduction in training volume of roughly 50% is used. If greater training loads precede the taper, then a greater reduction in volume may be needed. A non-progressive taper in which a faster, more considerable reduction in volume is seen, would warrant a shorter tapering period and specific fitness will be lost faster.

Frequency of Training

A greater tapering affect is typically seen when a large reduction in training frequency is not used. There will be a reduction in frequency but only slightly. Technical training and overall training frequency should be kept to around 80% of pre-tapering training.

Duration of the Taper

This is difficult to determine and depends on each athlete and the type of taper used. For the progressive taper used in this book a taper can typically last from 1-3 weeks. I like to use multiple short competition phases for this reason. The final taper for the peak competition will be similar and will be largely realized by the athlete's psychological state and technical proficiency at that time.

The below chart illustrates the differences between the taper and the previous phases of training.

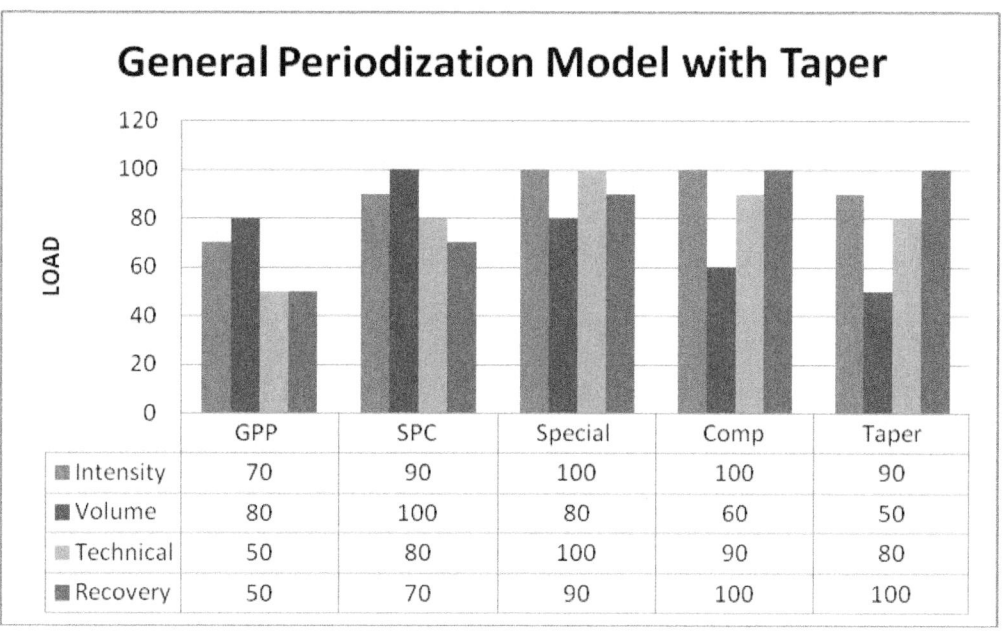

Graph 7.2

TAPERING GUIDELINES

- Slowly reduce training volume toward a taper
- The final taper affect should have a volume reduction of 50%
- Use the taper for 1-3 weeks at a time
- Keep training intensity and technical training frequency high
- Reduce overall training frequency by 20% during a taper
- Taper differently for important and non important competitions
- Only compete when the athlete is ready to achieve set goals for the specific competition
- Use multiple short competitive phases
- Avoid over competing
- Allow good training time between competitive phases
- Avoid setting high goals and achieving high arousal levels during non important competitions
- Expect a performance increase of 2-5% from a successful taper

Table 7.3

CHAPTER 7

SAMPLE TRAINING PROGRAMS

USA INFLUENCED PROGRAM

In this section are complete training blocks used within the yearly plan that utilize the principles explained throughout this book. The purpose of including such detailed examples is to demonstrate the principles discussed in their most important and relevant form so that all coaches and athletes can understand it. I cannot stress enough that these are examples of how each training phase could be performed. They are not, however, the only way they can be performed and used to develop the horizontal jumper.

The specific examples were successfully used with experienced jumpers who had developed high training ability over several years of training. The same programs used with less advanced athletes could result in overtraining, decreased performance and possibly even injury. For such athletes it would be necessary to decrease overall volume of training considerably and be sure that exercise choices reflect the athlete's technical and physical capability.

It is important that the athlete/coach understand a few general usage guidelines of the program before trying to implement a similar program. Firstly, these training programs work using the specific training inventory listed in Chapter 8. For example, if the program reads *Endurance Bounding A,* the coach/athlete will follow what is written on the training inventory under that heading. Another important factor is that these programs use AM and PM split routines.

The evening or second workout of the day is preferably performed at least 4 hours later. It is possible that the athlete performs a single session set-up while using the USA influenced program. If this is the case he/she can combine the track and weight training workout and decrease the overall volume of the day, especially during the weight room session.

Close attention should also be made to how the athlete is feeling prior to the weight training session. He/she will likely be slightly fatigued from the prior track session. Here, the athlete may decrease overall volume and/or intensity or change the type of weight training workout to one requiring less demand.

During a single session set-up like this it is even more important that the athlete remain hydrated and also snack on a protein or energy bar before the weight training section of the workout.

The competition schedule is another component of the program which can be manipulated in many ways. The athlete may have multiple competitions in a week or have a single competition which is on Wednesday.

During competition time, training load is very low with the most important outcome being a very sharp but rested athlete. To achieve this, training intensity and specificity must be high and training volume must be very low.

Some athletes need higher intensity stimulation the day before a competition and some need a rest day. This is unique to each athlete and can only be determined through experience. After the training program/season is complete a transition/active rest period of 4-6 weeks is recommended.

During the below section you will find the following types of sample training programs:

- USA Influence w/Flexible Non Linear Weight Training

- USA Influence OPTION B (Linear Weight Training w/alternate Plyometric split)

4 WEEK GENERAL PREPARATION – USA INFLUENCE NON-LINEAR

WEEK 1

Sunday	Wednesday
• 10 min easy jog warm up • Static flex B, Sprint drills B • 2 foot bunny hops – 6x 6 jumps • Power skips – no vest – 2x40m each • Standing Broad – 4x 5 jumps w/pause • Ankle series – 2x30 secs on/off	• 10 min easy jog warm up • Static flex B, Sprint drills B • Hopping series – 2x20m • Alt – Hill bounds/ flat bounds - 2x30m each • Vertical multi jumps – 4 ex/ 3x10 reps (Squat, Split, Tuck, S/L jump)

Monday	Thursday
• 15 min warm up (Jog, skip) • Static Flex A, Sprint drills A • Dynamic flex A • 2x4x15m sprints @100% PM) Weights: M • Dead lift – 4x6 @80% clean max • Squats – 4x8 @70% • Pull up – 3x8 • Reaching Lunges – 3x8+8	• 15 min warm up (Jog, skip) • Static Flex A, Dynam flex A • Sprint drills – 2x8x 50m • Hurdle drills – 2x6x6 ex PM) Weights: M • Squat Clean – 4x4 (2 @80%) • STOP squats – 4x6 @75% • Bent over rows – 3x10 • Step ups – 3x10 • RDL – 2x8

Tuesday	Friday
• 10 min jog on grass, Static flex • 10x100 strides on grass • Core Stability – Floor Series – 2x10 • Postural Series A – 2x15	• 15 min warm up (Jog, Skip) • Sprint drills A, Dynam flex A • Interval runs – Field Figure 8 – Run/jog x8 • Core stability – Ball series – 2x15 sec hold • Circuit Weights – 3x10x 12 reps • Postural Series B – 2x15

WEEK 2

Sunday	Wednesday
• 10 min easy jog warm up • Static flex B, Sprint drills B • 2 foot bunny hops – 6x 8 jumps • Power skips – no vest – 2x50m each • Standing Broad – 4x 5 jumps w/pause • Ankle series – 2x30 secs on/off	• 10 min easy jog warm up • Static flex B, Sprint drills B • Hopping series – 2x20m • Alt – Hill bounds/ flat bounds -2x40m each • Vertical multi jumps – 4 ex/ 3x15 reps (Squat, Split, Tuck, S/L jump)

Monday	Thursday
• 15 min warm up (Jog, skip) • Static Flex A, Sprint drills A • Dynamic flex A • 2x5x20m sprints @100% PM) Weights: M • Dead lift – 4x6 @85% clean max • Squats – 4x7 @75% • Pull up – 3x8 • Reaching Lunges – 3x8+8	• 15 min warm up (Jog, skip, etc) • Static Flex A, Dynamic flex A • Sprint drills – 2x8x 50m • Hurdle drills – 2x6x6 each PM) Weights: M • Power Clean – 4x4 (last 3 @80%) • STOP squats – 4x6 @77.5% • Bent over row – 3x10 • Step ups – 4x8 • RDL – 2x8

Tuesday	Friday
• 10 min jog on grass, static flex • 12x 100m strides on grass • Core stability – Floor series – 2x12 • Postural Series A – 2x15	• 15 min warm up (Jog, skip) • Dynam flex A, Hurdle drill B • Interval runs – Figure 8 – Run/jog x10 • Core stability – Ball series – 2x15 sec hold PM) Weights: L • Circuit Weights – 3x10x 12 reps • Postural Series B – 2x15

WEEK 3

Sunday	Wednesday
<ul><li>10 min easy jog warm up</li><li>Static flex B, Sprint drills B</li><li>2 foot bunny hops – 7x 8 jumps</li><li>Power skips – no vest – 3x50m each</li><li>Standing Broad – 4x 5 jumps w/pause</li><li>Ankle series – 2x30 secs on/off</li></ul>	<ul><li>10 min easy jog warm up</li><li>Static flex B, Sprint drills B</li><li>Hopping series – 2x20m</li><li>Alt – Hill bounds/ flat bounds -3x40m each</li><li>Vertical multi jumps – 4 ex/ 3x15 reps (Squat, Split, Tuck, S/L jump)</li></ul>

Monday	Thursday
<ul><li>15 min warm up (Jog, skip)</li><li>Static Flex A, Sprint drills A</li><li>Dynamic flex A</li><li>2x6x20m sprints @100%</li></ul> PM) Weights: M<ul><li>Dead lift – 4x6 @85% clean max</li><li>Squats – 4x7 @77.5%</li><li>Pull up – 3x8</li><li>Reaching Lunges – 3x8+8</li></ul>	<ul><li>15 min warm up (Jog, skip)</li><li>Static Flex A, Dynamic flex A</li><li>Sprint drills – 2x8x 50m</li><li>Hurdle drills – 2x6x6 each</li></ul> PM) Weights: M<ul><li>Power Clean – 4x4 (last 3 @82.5%)</li><li>STOP squats – 4x5 @80%</li><li>Bent over row – 3x10</li><li>Step ups – 4x8</li><li>RDL – 2x8</li></ul>

Tuesday	Friday
<ul><li>10 min jog on grass, static flex</li><li>14x 100m strides on grass</li><li>Core stability – Floor series – 2x12</li><li>Postural Series A – 2x15</li></ul>	<ul><li>15 min warm up (Jog, skip),</li><li>Sprint drills A , Dynamic Flex A</li><li>Hurdle drills B</li><li>Interval runs – Figure 8 – Run/jog x6</li><li>Core stability – Ball series – 2x15 sec hold</li></ul> PM) Weights: L<ul><li>Circuit Weights – 2x10x 12 reps</li><li>Postural Series B – 2x15</li></ul>

WEEK 4

Sunday
- 10 min easy jog warm up
- Static flex B, Sprint drills B
- SLJ TEST:
- 2 foot bunny hops – 6x 6 jumps
- Power skips – no vest – 4x40m

Monday
- 15 min warm up (Jog, skip, etc)
- Static Flex A, Sprint drills A
- Dynamic flex A
- 2x3x15m sprints @100%

PM) Weights: M
- Dead lift – 3x6 @70% clean max
- Squats TEST:
- Pull up – 2x8
- Reaching Lunges – 2x8+8

Tuesday
REST/Treatment

Wednesday
- 10 min easy jog warm up
- Static flex B, Sprint drills B
- Hopping series – 2x20m
- STJ TEST:
- 4 B+J TEST:
- Vertical multi jumps – 4 ex/ 2x10 reps (Squat, Split, Tuck S/L jump)

Thursday
- 15 min warm up (Jog, skip)
- Static Flex A, Sprint drills A
- Dynamic flex A
- 30 sprint TEST:
- Hurdle drills – 1x6x6 each

PM) Weights: H
- Power Clean TEST:
- STOP squats – 3x6 @70%
- Bent over row – 2x10
- Step ups – 2x10
- RDL – 2x8

Friday
- Short warm up, static flex
- Sprint drills, dynamic flex
- Interval runs – Figure 8 – Run/jog x6
- Core stability – Ball series – 2x15 sec hold\

PM) Weights: L
- Circuit Weights – 2x10 x12reps
- Postural Series A – 2x15

3 WEEK SPC - USA INFLUENCED NON-LINEAR

WEEK 1

Sunday	Wednesday
<ul><li>10 min easy jog warm up</li><li>Static flex B, Sprint drills B</li><li>Hurdle drills A – 6 hurdles</li><li>Short approach jumps w/vest – 5x5 strides</li><li>Short approach jumps – 5x9 strides</li><li>Specific Bounding C – x2</li><li>Ankle series – 30s on/off</li></ul>	<ul><li>Short warm up, Static Flex A</li><li>Sprint drills A, Dynamic flex A</li><li>8x alt (20m fly & full approach)</li><li>Depth jump to hurdle hops – 5x6h</li><li>Ballistic – BLV + BLF – 4x5 each</li></ul> PM) Weights: L<ul><li>Step up – 2x10</li><li>Incline bench – 2x10</li><li>Seated row + Shoulder press – 2x10</li><li>Hamstring curl – 2x10</li><li>Upright row + Lat pull down – 2x10</li><li>Calf raise – 2x10</li></ul>
Monday	Thursday
<ul><li>Short warm up, Static Flex A</li><li>Sprint drills A, Dynamic flex A</li><li>3x (30,40,50m) sprints</li><li>Endurance bounding A – x2 (grass)</li></ul> PM) Weights: H<ul><li>Power Clean – 6x3 (last 4 @85%)</li><li>ECC squats – 5x5 @60% (SLOW)</li><li>Bench press – 3x4 (last 4 @85%)</li><li>Seated Row + Shoulder press – 3x6</li><li>RDL – 2x8</li><li>ECC calf – 2x8</li></ul>	<ul><li>10 min easy jog warm up</li><li>Static flex B, Sprint drills B</li><li>Tempo – 14x100m strides on grass</li><li>Postural Series A – 2x15</li></ul>
Tuesday	Friday
REST	<ul><li>Short warm up, Sprint drills A</li><li>Dynamic flex A</li><li>2x3x 150m (30m @95% + float) w/4/8 rec</li><li>4BJ w/2 run in strides – x4</li></ul> PM) Weights: VH<ul><li>Hang Clean – 2x2, 5x1 @95%</li><li>Bench – 4x2 @90%</li><li>Bulgarian Squat – 6x3 (4 @85%)</li><li>Resisted Pull ups – 4x6</li></ul>

WEEK 2

Sunday	Wednesday
<ul><li>Short warm up</li><li>Static flex B, Sprint drills B</li><li>Hurdle drills A – 6 hurdles</li><li>Short approach jumps w/vest – 4x5 strides</li><li>Short approach jumps – 2x9, 2x11 strides</li><li>Specific bounding C – x1</li><li>Ankle series – 30s on/off</li></ul>	<ul><li>Short warm up, Static Flex A</li><li>Sprint drills A, Dynamic flex A</li><li>6x alt (20m fly & full approach w/pop)</li><li>Depth jump (45cm) to hurdle hops – 4x6h</li></ul> PM) Weights: VH<ul><li>Hang Clean – 2x2, 4x1 @90%</li><li>Bench – 3x2@ 87.5%</li><li>Bulgarian Squat – 5x3 (last 3 @85%)</li><li>Resisted pull ups – 3x6</li></ul>
Monday	**Thursday**
<ul><li>Short warm up, Static Flex A</li><li>Sprint drills A, Dynamic flex A</li><li>3x (40m, 50m) sprints</li><li>Endurance bounding A – x2 (grass)</li><li>Ballistic – BLV + BLF – 3x5 each</li></ul> PM) Weights: L<ul><li>Step up – 2x10</li><li>Incline bench – 2x10</li><li>Seated row + Shoulder press – 2x10</li><li>Leg curl – 2x10</li><li>Upright row + Lat pull down – 2x10</li><li>Calf raise – 2x10</li></ul>	<ul><li>10 min easy jog warm up</li><li>Static flex B, Sprint drills B</li><li>Ext Tempo – 12x100m strides on grass</li><li>Postural Series A – 2x15</li></ul>
Tuesday	**Friday**
REST	<ul><li>Short warm up, Sprint drills A</li><li>Dynamic flex A</li><li>5x 150m (40m @95% + float) w/4/8 rec</li><li>4BJ w/2 stride run in – x3</li></ul> PM) Weights: M 1. Hang Clean – 4x4 @75% 2. Parallel Squat – 3x6 @75% 3. Bench press – 3x6 @75% 4. Seated Row + Shoulder press – 2x8 5. Back ext – 3x10

WEEK 3

Monday	Wednesday
<ul><li>10 min easy jog warm up</li><li>Static flex B, Sprint drills B</li><li>Hurdle drills A – 6 hurdles</li><li>TEST: 12 stride long/triple jump</li><li>Ankle series – 30s on/off</li></ul>	<ul><li>Short warm up, Sprint drills A</li><li>Dynamic flex A</li><li>TEST: 30m sprint</li><li>TEST: 150m</li></ul> PM) Weights: M<ul><li>Power Clean – TEST</li><li>Max Vertical - TEST</li><li>DEEP Squat – 3x6 @70%</li><li>Seated Row + Shoulder press – 3x8</li></ul>
Monday	**Thursday**
<ul><li>Short warm up, Static Flex A</li><li>Sprint drills A, Dynamic flex A</li><li>5x30m sprints</li><li>TEST: STJ, 4BJ</li></ul> PM) Weights: H<ul><li>Power Clean – 4x2 (last 2 @85%)</li><li>Parallel squat - TEST</li><li>Bench press – TEST</li><li>Pull ups – 3x6</li></ul>	REST
Tuesday	**Friday**
REST	<ul><li>Short warm up, Static Flex A</li><li>Sprint drills A, Dynamic flex A</li><li>3x (40m sprints + Full approaches)</li><li>Depth to hurdle hops – 3x6</li></ul> PM) Weights: VL - (1x 15 reps @light weight)<ul><li>Squat, Bench</li><li>Seated row, Sit ups</li><li>Back hyper, Leg Ext</li><li>Calf raise, Shoulder press</li><li>Arm curl</li></ul>

3 WEEK TECHNICAL TRAINING – USA INFLUENCE NON-LINEAR

WEEK 1

Sunday
- 10 min easy jog warm up
- Static flex B, Sprint drills B
- Hurdle drills A – 6 hurdles
- Short approach jumps – 9,11,9,11,9,11
- Total body series – 2x12
- Ankle series – 30s on/off

Monday
- Short warm up, Static Flex A
- Sprint drills A, Dynamic flex A
- 3x2x 40m sprints (5/8 min rec)
- Max 4 Bounds + Jumps – x4

PM) Weights: P
- Power clean – 8x2 @80%
- Fast box strikes – 4x6 @35%
- Bench press – 4x6 @70%
- MB throw: 2x6 w/4 run in strides
- Hanging abs – 3x6

Tuesday

REST

Wednesday
- Short warm up, Sprint drills A
- Dynamic flex A, Hurdle Drills B
- Full approaches – x6
- Short approach jumps – 4x13 strides
- Box jump B – 4x3

PM) Weights: P
- Split Snatch – 8x2 @45%
- Jump squats – 4x6 @35%
+
- Stiff box drops (90cm) – x5
- Clap pull ups – 4x6
- Hanging abs – 3x6

Thursday
- 10 min easy jog warm up, Static flex B
- Sprint drills B
- Ext Tempo – 16x100m strides on grass
- Postural Series A – 2x15

Friday
- Short warm up, Static Flex A,
- Sprint drills A, Dynamic flex A
- 3x 5 hurdle hops into 20m sprint
- 4x10m fly sprints
- Speed End: 1x150m sprints @90%

PM) Weights: L
- S/L Squat – 2x10
- Incline bench – 2x10
- Seated row + Shoulder press – 2x10
- Leg curl – 2x10
- Upright row + Lat pull down – 2x10

WEEK 2

Sunday

- 10 min easy jog warm up
- Static flex B, Sprint drills B
- Hurdle drills A – 6 hurdles
- Short approach jumps – 9,11,11,9,11,11
- Total body series – 2x12
- Ankle series – 30s on/off

Monday

- Short warm up, Static Flex A
- Sprint drills A, Dynamic flex A
- 2x2x50m sprints w/6/10 min rec
- 6 stride 4BJ – x3

PM) Weights: P
- Hang Snatch – 6x2 @45%
- S/L fast squats – 4x6 @20%
- Drop push-ups – 4x6
- MB Throw: 2x5 w/4 run in strides
- Hanging abs – 3x6

Tuesday

REST

Wednesday

- Short warm up, Sprint drills A
- Dynamic flex A, Hurdle Drills B
- Full approaches – 5
- Short approach jumps – 3x13 strides
- Box jump B – 3x3

PM) Weights: P
- Hang clean – 5x3 @75%
- Jump squats – 4x6 @30%
  +
- Stiff box drops (90cm) x5
- Bench press - 4x6 @45%
- Clap pull ups – 3x6

Thursday

- 10 min easy jog warm up
- Static flex B, Sprint drills B
- Ext Tempo – 14x100m strides on grass
- Postural Series B – 2x15

Friday

- Short warm up, Static Flex A
- Sprint drills A, Dynamic flex A
- 3x5x hurdle hops into 20m sprint
- 3x10m fly sprints
- Speed End: 1x150m sprints

PM) Weights: L
- S/L Squat – 2x10
- Incline bench – 2x10
- Seated row + Shoulder press – 2x10
- Leg curl – 2x10
- Upright row + Lat pull down – 2x1

WEEK 3

Sunday

- 10 min easy jog warm up
- Static flex B, Sprint drills B
- Hurdle drills A – 6 hurdles
- 13 stride LJ TEST:
- Max 4 Bounds + Jump TEST:
- Core Stability – 20 mins

Monday

- Short warm up, Static Flex A
- Sprint drills A, Dynamic flex A
- 5x30m sprints

PM) Weights: H
- Power Clean – 4x2 (last 2 @85%)
- Parallel Squat TEST:
- Jump squats – 3x6 @30%
- Bench – 5,4,3

Tuesday

REST

Wednesday

- Short warm up, Static flex
- Sprint drills, dynamic flex
- 8x100m strides
- GS: Total body, Core stability

Thursday

- Short warm up, Sprint drills A
- Dynamic flex A, Hurdle Drills B
- TEST: 40m sprints
- TEST: Full Approach – 11m-1m

PM) Weights: P
- Power Clean TEST:
- Jump squats – 4x6 @40%
  +
- Stiff box drops (90cm) x5
- Bench – 6x4 @80%
- Stiff jumps – 3x8

Friday

REST

3 WEEK SPC – USA INFLUENCE OPTION B

WEEK 1

Sunday	Wednesday
<ul><li>10 min easy jog warm up</li><li>Static flex B, Sprint drills B</li><li>Hurdle drills A – 6 hurdles</li><li>Short approach jump – (9,11,9,11,9,11)</li><li>Ankle series – 30s on/off</li></ul>PM) Weights:<ul><li>Power Clean – 6x3 (last 4 @85%)</li><li>Eccentric squats – 3x1 @100%</li><li>Squats – 3x3 @70%</li><li>Pushups w/vest – 4x15</li><li>RDL – 2x8</li></ul>	<ul><li>Short warm up</li><li>Static Flex A, Sprint drills A</li><li>Hurdle drills A – 6 hurdles</li><li>1-2-3 drill – 4x40m</li><li>Landing/ Flight drills (20 mins)</li></ul>PM) Weights:<ul><li>Power Snatch – 6x2 (Last 3 @90%)</li><li>Step ups – 4x5 @heavy</li><li>Incline pushups w/vest – 4x15</li><li>+ Pull ups – x10</li><li>Reaching lunges – 2x8 EL @light weight</li></ul>
Monday	Thursday
<ul><li>Short warm up, Static Flex A</li><li>Sprint drills A, Dynamic flex A</li><li>3x2x40m sprints</li><li>Depth jumps OR S/L depth jumps – Alt vest/no vest – 2x5 each</li><li>Standing 4BJ – Alt vest/ no vest – x3 each</li><li>Combination Bounding – 4x40m</li></ul>	<ul><li>10 min jog warm up, Static flex B</li><li>Sprint drills B</li><li>4 x full approaches on the track</li><li>4x 60m sprints</li><li>Hurdle hops – Alt vest/no vest – 2x5 hurdles each</li><li>Standing 4HJ – x3 each leg</li><li>Alt Bounding – 4x40m</li></ul>
Tuesday	Friday
REST	<ul><li>Short warm up, Sprint drills A</li><li>Dynamic flex A</li><li>2x3x 175m sprints @75% w/4/8 min rec</li><li>Weight circuit LONG – 3x12</li></ul>

WEEK 2

Sunday	Wednesday
<ul><li>10 min easy jog warm up</li><li>Static flex B, Sprint drills B</li><li>Hurdle drills A – 6 hurdles</li><li>Short approach jump – (11,11,9,11,11)</li><li>Ankle series – 30s on/off</li></ul>PM) Weights:<ul><li>Power Clean – 5x3 (last 2 @85%)</li><li>Eccentric squats – 3x1 @100%</li><li>Squats – 3x3 @70%</li><li>Pushups w/vest – 4x15</li><li>RDL – 2x8</li></ul>	<ul><li>Short warm up</li><li>Static Flex A, Sprint drills A</li><li>Sprint drills A – 6 hurdles</li><li>1-2-3 drill – 4x40m</li><li>Landing/ Flight drills (20 mins)</li></ul>PM) Weights:<ul><li>Power Snatch – 5x2 (Last 3 @90%)</li><li>Step ups – 4x5 @heavy</li><li>Incline pushups w/vest – 4x15</li><li>+ Pull ups – x10</li><li>Reaching lunges – 2x8 EL @light weight</li></ul>
Monday	**Thursday**
<ul><li>Short warm up, Static Flex A</li><li>Sprint drills A, Dynamic flex A</li><li>2x2x50m sprints</li><li>Depth jumps OR S/L depth jumps – Alt vest/no vest – 2x5 each</li><li>Standing 4BJ – Alt vest/ no vest – x3 each</li><li>Combination Bounding – 4x40m</li></ul>	<ul><li>10 min easy jog warm up, Static flex B</li><li>Sprint drills B</li><li>3 x full approaches on the track</li><li>3x 60m sprints</li><li>Hurdle hops – Alt vest/no vest – 2x5 hurdles each</li><li>Standing 4HJ – x3 each leg</li><li>Alt Bounding – 4x40m</li></ul>
Tuesday	**Friday**
REST	<ul><li>Short warm up, Sprint drills A</li><li>Dynamic flex A</li><li>2x2x 175m sprints @75% w/4/8 min rec</li><li>Weight circuit LONG – 3x12</li></ul>

WEEK 3

Sunday	Wednesday
<ul><li>10 min easy jog warm up</li><li>Static flex B, Sprint drills B</li><li>Hurdle drills A – 6 hurdles</li><li>11 stride LJ TEST:</li><li>4Bounds + Jump TEST:</li><li>Core Stability – 20 mins</li><li>Ankle series – 30s on/off</li></ul>	<ul><li>Short warm up, Static flex</li><li>Sprint drills, dynamic flex</li><li>8x100m strides</li><li>GS: Total body, Core stability</li></ul>

Monday	Thursday
<ul><li>Short warm up, Static Flex A</li><li>Sprint drills A, Dynamic flex A</li><li>5x40m sprints</li></ul>PM) Weights: H<ul><li>Power Clean – 4x2 (last 2 @85%)</li><li>Parallel Squat TEST:</li><li>Jump squats – 3x6 @30%</li><li>Bench – 5,4,3</li></ul>	<ul><li>Short warm up, Sprint drills A</li><li>Dynamic flex A, Hurdle Drills B</li><li>TEST: 40m sprints</li><li>TEST: Fly 10m</li></ul>PM) Weights: P<ul><li>Power Clean TEST:</li><li>Jump squats – 4x6 @40% +</li><li>Stiff box drops (90cm) x5</li><li>Bench – 6x4 @80%</li><li>Stiff jumps – 3x8</li></ul>

Tuesday	Friday
REST	REST

3 WEEK TECHNICAL TRAINING – USA INFLUENCE OPTION B

WEEK 1

Sunday	Wednesday
<ul><li>10 min easy jog warm up</li><li>Static flex B, Sprint drills B</li><li>Hurdle drills A – 6 hurdles</li><li>Short approach jumps – 6x13 strides</li><li>Total body series – 2x12</li><li>Ankle series – 30s on/off</li></ul>PM) Weights:<ul><li>Split clean – 4x2 @85, 87.5, 90, 80%</li><li>½ Squats – 4x2 @85, 90, 90, 80%</li><li>Kipping pull ups – 4x6</li><li>Back Ext – 3x10</li></ul>	<ul><li>Short warm up, Sprint drills A</li><li>Dynamic flex A, Hurdle Drills B</li><li>Landing/ Flight drills (20 mins)</li><li>Short approach jumps – 7,9,7,9,7,9 strides</li></ul>PM) Weights:<ul><li>Hang clean – 6x2 @75% FAST</li><li>Dynamic step ups – 4x6 @25% FAST</li><li>Bench press – 3x6 @45% FAST</li><li>Jump squats – 3x6 @30%</li></ul>
Monday	**Thursday**
<ul><li>Short warm up, Static Flex A</li><li>Sprint drills A, Dynamic flex A</li><li>4x approach rhythm sprints</li><li>30,40,50,60m sprints</li><li>MB throw: 2x6</li><li>High Shock Depth jumps – 3x3</li><li>Max 4 Bounds + Jumps – x4</li><li>Speed bounding – 4x20m</li></ul>	<ul><li>10 min easy jog warm up</li><li>Static flex B, Sprint drills B</li><li>Full approaches w/ pop up – x4-6</li><li>Fly 20m sprints x2-4</li><li>Hurdle hops – 4x5 hurdles</li><li>Max 4 Hops + Jump – x2 each leg</li><li>Speed Hopping – 2x20m each leg</li></ul>
Tuesday	**Friday**
REST	<ul><li>Short warm up, Sprint drills A</li><li>Dynamic flex A</li><li>6x 150m sprints @75% w/3 min rec</li><li>Weight circuit Short – 3x10</li></ul>

WEEK 2

Sunday	Wednesday
<ul><li>10 min easy jog warm up</li><li>Static flex B, Sprint drills B</li><li>Hurdle drills A – 6 hurdles</li><li>Short approach jumps – 4x15 strides</li><li>Total body series – 2x12</li><li>Ankle series – 30s on/off</li></ul>PM) Weights:<ul><li>Split clean – 4x2 @70% FAST</li><li>Speed Squats – 4x6 @50%</li><li>Resisted pull ups – 4x6</li><li>Back Ext – 3x10</li></ul>	<ul><li>Short warm up, Sprint drills A</li><li>Dynamic flex A, Hurdle Drills B</li><li>Landing/ Flight drills (20 mins)</li><li>Short approach jumps – 4x9 strides</li></ul>PM) Weights:<ul><li>Hang clean – 4x2 @75% FAST</li><li>Dynamic step ups – 3x6 @25% FAST</li><li>Bench press – 3x6 @45% FAST</li><li>Jump squats – 3x6 @30%</li></ul>
Monday	**Thursday**
<ul><li>Short warm up, Static Flex A</li><li>Sprint drills A, Dynamic flex A</li><li>4x approach rhythm sprints</li><li>3x60m sprints</li><li>MB throw: 2x6</li><li>High Shock Depth jumps – 3x3</li><li>Max 4BJ – x4</li><li>Speed bounding – 4x20m</li></ul>	<ul><li>10 min easy jog warm up</li><li>Static flex B, Sprint drills B</li><li>Full approaches w/ pop up – x3</li><li>Fly 20m sprints x3</li><li>Hurdle hops – 3x5 hurdles</li><li>Max 4HJ – x2 each leg</li><li>Speed Hopping – 2x20m each leg</li></ul>
Tuesday	**Friday**
REST	<ul><li>Short warm up, Sprint drills A</li><li>Dynamic flex A</li><li>4x 150m sprints @75% w/3 min rec</li><li>Weight circuit SHORT – 3x10</li></ul>

WEEK 3

Sunday	Wednesday
<ul><li>10 min easy jog warm up</li><li>Static flex B, Sprint drills B</li><li>Hurdle drills A – 6 hurdles</li><li>13 stride LJ TEST:</li><li>MAX 4Bounds + Jump TEST:</li><li>Core Stability – 20 mins</li><li>Ankle series – 30s on/off</li></ul>	<ul><li>Short warm up, Static flex</li><li>Sprint drills, dynamic flex</li><li>8x100m strides</li><li>GS: Total body, Core stability</li></ul>

Monday	Thursday
<ul><li>Short warm up, Static Flex A</li><li>Sprint drills A, Dynamic flex A</li><li>5x30m sprints</li></ul>PM) Weights: H<ul><li>Power Clean – 4x2 (last 2 @85%)</li><li>Parallel Squat TEST:</li><li>Jump squats – 3x6 @30%</li><li>Bench – 5,4,3</li></ul>	<ul><li>Short warm up, Sprint drills A</li><li>Dynamic flex A, Hurdle Drills B</li><li>TEST: 40m sprints</li><li>TEST: Full Approach – 11m-1m</li></ul>PM) Weights: P<ul><li>Power Clean TEST:</li><li>Jump squats – 4x6 @40% +</li><li>Stiff box drops (90cm) x5</li><li>Bench – 6x4 @80%</li><li>Stiff jumps – 3x8</li></ul>

Tuesday	Friday
REST	REST

EXAMPLE OF EARLY SEASON COMPETITION WEEK – USA INFLUENCE

Sunday	Thursday
<ul><li>Slow warm up, static flex</li><li>Hurdle drills – 2x6x6</li><li>Short approach jumps – 6x13 strides</li><li>Ankle series – 2x 30 secs on/off</li></ul>	<ul><li>Short warm up, static flex</li><li>Sprint drills, dynamic flex</li><li>10x 100m strides on grass</li><li>GS: Core stability – 3x20 sec hold</li></ul>

Monday	Friday
<ul><li>Short warm up, static flex</li><li>Sprint drills, dynamic flex</li><li>Fly 20m sprints x4</li><li>2x120m sprints</li></ul> PM) Weights: <ul><li>Cleans – 2x2, 4x1 @85%</li><li>Squats – 4x4 @80% FAST +</li><li>Depth jump – x5</li><li>Bench – 3x5 @ build up</li></ul>	<ul><li>Short warm up, static flex</li><li>Sprint drills, dynamic flex</li><li>4x20m sprints</li><li>Hurdle hops - 3x5</li></ul>

Wednesday	Saturday
<ul><li>Short warm up, static flex</li><li>Sprint drills, dynamic flex</li><li>Full approach runs – x6</li><li>4BJ x4 w/4 stride run in</li></ul> PM) Weights: <ul><li>Hang Cleans – 4x3 @75%</li><li>Stiff jumps – 4x6</li><li>Kippin Pull ups – 3x6</li></ul>	<ul><li>Competition</li></ul>

EXAMPLE OF MAIN SEASON COMPETITION WEEK – USA INFLUENCE

Sunday	Thursday
<ul><li>Slow warm up, static flex</li><li>Hurdle drills – 2x6x6</li><li>Short approach jumps – 6x11 strides</li><li>Ankle series – 2x 30 secs on/off</li></ul>	<ul><li>Short warm up, static flex</li><li>Sprint drills, dynamic flex</li><li>4x15, 3x25, 4x35m sprints</li></ul>Weights:<ul><li>Hang Cleans – 4x3 @70%</li><li>Stiff jumps – 3x8</li></ul>
Monday	**Friday**
<ul><li>Short warm up, static flex</li><li>Sprint drills, dynamic flex</li><li>Fly 10m sprints x4</li><li>2x90m sprints</li></ul>PM) Weights:<ul><li>Cleans – 2x2, 4x1 @80%</li><li>Jump squats – 3x5 @30% FAST +</li><li>Depth jump – x5</li><li>Bench – 3x5 @ build up</li></ul>	<ul><li>Short warm up, static flex</li><li>Sprint drills, dynamic flex</li><li>5x50m easy build ups</li></ul>
Wednesday	**Saturday**
REST	<ul><li>Competition</li></ul>

EXAMPLE OF PEAK SEASON COMPETITION WEEK – USA INFLUENCE

Sunday	Thursday
<ul><li>Slow warm up, static flex</li><li>Hurdle drills – 2x5x5</li><li>10x100m strides on grass</li><li>GS: Core stability – 2x20 sec hold</li></ul>	<ul><li>Short warm up, static flex</li><li>Sprint drills, dynamic flex</li><li>4x15, 3x25, 4x35m sprints</li></ul> Weights: <ul><li>Hang Cleans – 4x3 @70%</li><li>Stiff jumps – 3x8</li></ul>
Monday	**Friday**
<ul><li>Short warm up, static flex</li><li>Sprint drills, dynamic flex</li><li>Fly 10m sprints x4</li><li>2x60m sprints</li></ul> PM) Weights: <ul><li>Cleans – 2x2, 4x1 @80%</li><li>Jump squats – 3x5 @30% FAST +</li><li>Depth jump – x5</li><li>Bench – 3x5 @ build up</li></ul>	<ul><li>Short warm up, static flex</li><li>Sprint drills, dynamic flex</li><li>5x50m easy build ups</li></ul>
Wednesday	**Saturday**
<ul><li>Short warm up, static flex</li><li>Hurdle drills – 2x4x4</li><li>6x100m strides on grass</li></ul>	<ul><li>Competition</li></ul>

EUROPEAN INFLUENCED PROGRAM

As discussed earlier, this particular set-up differs greatly from the USA influenced program. The major training components of the two set-ups are however very similar and mainly differ only with the way they are arranged during each week. Although this set-up is very effective it can be tough for many athletes to handle.

The repetitive high intensity training day in day out can be very physically and mentally demanding. In my experience, however, I will say that most athletes I have worked with enjoy this set-up the most because of its high intensity nature. Most enjoy the "important" sessions the most so this set-up makes every day fun and challenging.

It is especially important with this set-up that the lower intensity general strength and fitness training is maintained throughout the year. These sessions greatly enhance recovery and will become essential for injury prevention. Another important factor when programming the European Influenced set-up is to understand when to alter a prescribed session based the athlete's physical and mental readiness. There are no set-in-stone ways of doing this and what works best is largely determined by the tendencies of the individual athlete.

In general, performing workouts such as light weight circuits, extensive tempo running, jogging on grass, pool workouts and other low intensity training will aid recovery and be a great substitute for an overly fatigued athlete. It is recommended that anytime the athlete feels significantly flat or fatigued, he/she should substitute with a recovery based workout.

In the following section European Influence w/ Linear Weight Training sample programs.

4 WEEK GENERAL PREPARATION – EUROPEAN INFLUENCE
WEEK 1

Sunday
- 10 min easy jog warm up
- Static flex B, Sprint drills B
- 2 foot bunny hops – 5x 6 jumps
- Power skips – 4x30m
- SLJ – 3x 5 jumps w/ pause
- Hopping series B – 2x20m
- Circuit Weights LONG – 2x12
- Core stability – Hold – 2x20 sec

Wednesday
- 10 min easy jog warm up
- Static flex B, Sprint drills B
- Hopping series A – 2x20m
- Alternate bounding - 4x30m
- Vertical multi jumps – 4 ex/2x10 reps (Squat, Split, Tuck, S/L jump)
- Circuit Weights LONG – 2x12
- Core stability – REP – 2x 10 rep

Monday
- 15 min warm up (Jog, skip, etc)
- Static Flex A, Sprint drills A
- Dynamic flex A
- 2x4x20m sprints @100%
- Core series – x3
- Core Stability – Reps – 2x12

Thursday
- 15 min warm up (Jog, skip, etc)
- Static Flex A, Dynamic flex A
- Sprint drills – 2x8x 40m (SHARP)
- 6x100m strides @80%
- Hurdle drills – 2x6x6 ex
- Core series – x3
- Core stability – HOLD – 2x20 sec

Tuesday
- Dead lift – 3x6 @70% clean max
- DEEP Squats – 3x8 @70%
- Pull up – 3x10
- Reaching Lunges – 3x10 el

Friday
- Squat Clean – 4x6 (last 2 @70%)
- STOP squats – 3x8 @70%
- Bent over rows – 3x10
- Step ups – 2x10
- RDL – 2x8

WEEK 2

Sunday

- 10 min easy jog warm up
- Static flex B, Sprint drills B
- 2 foot bunny hops – 5x10 jumps
- Power skips – 4x40m
- SLJ – 4x 5 jumps w/ pause
- Hopping series B – 2x20m
- Circuit Weights LONG – 2x12
- Core stability – Hold – 2x20 sec

Wednesday

- 10 min easy jog warm up
- Static flex B, Sprint drills B
- Hopping series A – 2x20m
- Alt bounding - 5x40m
- Vertical multi jumps – 4 ex/ 3x10 reps (Squat, Split, Tuck, S/L jump)
- Circuit Weights LONG – 2x12
- Core stability – REP – 2x 10 rep

Monday

- 15 min warm up (Jog, skip, etc)
- Static Flex A, Sprint drills A
- Dynamic flex A
- 2x5x20m sprints @100%
- Core series – x3
- Core stability – reps – 2x15

Thursday

- 15 min warm up (Jog, skip, etc)
- Static Flex A, Dynamic flex A
- Sprint drills – 2x8x 50m (SHARP)
- 8x100m strides @80%
- Hurdle drills – 2x6x6 ex
- Core series – x3
- Core stability – HOLD – 2x25 sec

Tuesday

- Dead lift – 4x6 @75% clean max
- DEEP Squats – 4x8 @72.5%
- Pull up – 3x10
- Reaching Lunges – 3x9 el

Friday

- Squat Clean – 5x6 (3@72.5%)
- STOP squats – 4x8 @70%
- Bent over rows – 3x10
- Step ups – 3x9
- RDL – 2x8

WEEK 3

Sunday

- 10 min easy jog warm up
- Static flex B, Sprint drills B
- 2 foot bunny hops – 5x 12 jumps
- Short approach jumps – 2x7, 2x9 strides
- Power skips – 4x50m
- SLJ– 4x 5 jumps w/ pause
- Hopping series B – 2x20m
- Circuit Weights LONG – 2x12
- Core stability – Hold – 2x20 sec

Wednesday

- 10 min easy jog warm up
- Static flex B, Sprint drills B
- Hopping series A – 2x20m
- Alt bounding - 6x50m
- Vertical multi jumps – 4 ex/ 3x10 reps (Squat, Split, Tuck, S/L jump)
- Circuit Weights LONG – 2x12
- Core stability – REP – 2x 10 rep

Monday

- 15 min warm up (Jog, skip, etc)
- Static Flex A, Sprint drills A
- Dynamic flex A
- 2x6x20m sprints @100%
- Core series – x3
- Core stability – Reps – 2x15

Thursday

- 15 min warm up (Jog, skip, etc)
- Static Flex A, Dynamic A
- Sprint drills – 2x8x 60m (SHARP)
- 10x 100m strides @70%
- Hurdle drills – 2x6x6 ex
- Core series – x3
- Core stability – HOLD – 2x20 sec

Tuesday

- Dead lift – 5x6 @80% clean max
- DEEP Squats – 5x8 @75%
- Pull up – 3x10
- Reaching Lunges – 3x8 el

Friday

- Squat Clean – 3x6 (last 1 @75%)
- STOP squats – 3x8 @75%
- Bent over rows – 3x10
- Step ups – 2x8
- RDL – 2x8

WEEK 4

Sunday	Wednesday
<ul><li>10 min easy jog warm up</li><li>Static flex B, Sprint drills B</li><li>9 stride LJ TEST:</li><li>4 Bounds +Jump TEST:</li><li>Circuit Weights SHORT – 2x12</li><li>Core stability – Hold – 2x20 sec</li></ul>	<ul><li>Short warm up , Static Flex A</li><li>Sprint drills A, Dynamic flex A</li><li>30 sprint TEST:</li><li>10 bounds TEST:</li><li>Hurdle drills – 1x6x6 each</li><li>Core series – x2</li></ul>

Monday	Thursday
<ul><li>15 min warm up (Jog, skip, etc)</li><li>Static Flex A, Sprint drills A</li><li>Dynamic flex A</li><li>2x3x20m sprints @100%</li><li>Core series – x2</li></ul>	<ul><li>Power Clean TEST:</li><li>Parallel Squat TEST:</li><li>Pull up – 2x8</li><li>Reaching Lunges – 2x8</li></ul>

Tuesday	Friday
REST	REST

3 WEEK SPC – EUROPEAN INFLUENCE

WEEK 1

Sunday	Wednesday
• 10 min easy jog warm up • Static flex B, Sprint drills B • Short approach jumps – 2x (9,11,9) Specific Bounding: • Depth jumps – vest - 3x5 (30cm box) • Standing 4 Bounds + Jump – x6 • Med ball circuit – 2x 10 reps • Core stability – Hold – 2x30 sec	• Short warm up • Static Flex A, Sprint drills A • LJ drills – Obstacle jump/ Landing • Hurdle jumps – vest – 4x5 Endurance Bounding: • Power skips – 4x50m • Combo Bounding – 4x40m • Circuit Weights LONG – 2x10 • Core stability – REP – 2x 15 rep

Monday	Thursday
• Short warm up, Static Flex A • Sprint drills A. Dynamic flex A • 2x4x40m sprints (Alt vest) • Hurdle drills – 2x6x6 each • Advanced Core series – x3	• 10 min easy jog , Static flex B • Sprint drills B, dynamic flex • 6 x Track approaches – Vary start 30-60cm • 2x60m sprints • Hurdle drills – 2x6x6 each • Advanced Core series – x3

Tuesday	Friday
• Power Clean – 6x4 (3 @80-85%) • Eccentric squats – 3x1 @100% + • Squats – 3x6 @75% • Resisted Pull ups – 3x8 • Standing Lunge – 2x6	• Split Clean – 6x4 Last 3 @75% • ¼ Squat – 4x5 @90% Parallel squat max • Bent over rows – 3x8 • Step ups – 4x6 @build up • MB THROW A – 2x3 w/15lb ball • RDL – 2x5

WEEK 2

Sunday	Wednesday
• 10 min easy jog warm up • Static flex B, Sprint drills B • Short approach jumps – 2x (9,11,11) - Specific Bounding: • Depth jumps - vest – 3x5 (30cm) • Standing 4 Bounds + Jump – x5 • Med ball circuit – 2x 10 reps • Core stability – Hold – 2x30 sec	• Short warm up • Static Flex A, Sprint drills A • LJ Drills – Obstacle jump/Landing • Hurdle jumps – vest – 3x5 each Endurance Bounding: • Power skips – 3x50m • Combo bounding – 3x40m • Circuit Weights LONG – 2x10 • Core stability – REP – 2x 15 rep
Monday	Thursday
• Short warm up, Static Flex A • Sprint drills A. Dynamic flex A • 2x3x40m sprints – (Alt vest) • Hurdle drills – 2x6x6 each • Advanced Core series – x3	• 10 min easy jog , Static flex B • Sprint drills B • 4 x Track approaches – Vary start 30-60cm • 2-4x60m sprints • Hurdle drills – 2x6x6 each • Advanced Core series – x3
Tuesday	Friday
• Clean – 5x3 (last 3 @85%) • Eccentric squats – 3x1 @110% + • Squats – 3x6 @75% • Resisted Pull ups – 3x8 • Standing Lunge – 3x6	• Split Clean – 4x4 Last 2 @80% • ¼ Squat – 3x5 @100% Parallel squat max • Bent over rows – 3x8 • Step ups –2x6 @build up • MB THROW A – 2x3 w/15lb ball • RDL – 2x6

WEEK 3

Sunday	Wednesday
<ul><li>10 min easy jog warm up</li><li>Static flex B, Sprint drills B</li><li>11 stride LJ TEST:</li><li>Standing 4Bounds + Jump TEST:</li><li>Med ball circuit – 2x 10 reps</li><li>Core stability – Hold – 2x30 sec</li></ul>	<ul><li>10 min easy jog warm up</li><li>Static flex B, Sprint drills B</li><li>30m sprint TEST:</li><li>Fly 11m sprint TEST:</li><li>Max 4 Bounds + Jump TEST:</li><li>Core series – x2</li></ul>

Monday	Thursday
<ul><li>Short warm up, Static Flex A</li><li>Sprint drills A, Dynamic flex A</li><li>5x30m sprints</li></ul>Weights:<ul><li>Power Clean - 4x3 @80%</li><li>Squat TEST:</li><li>Bent over row - 3x6</li><li>Step ups – 2x6</li><li>Core series – x2</li></ul>	<ul><li>Power Clean TEST:</li><li>Max Vertical jump TEST:</li><li>Resisted pull ups – 2x8</li><li>MB THROW A – 2x3 w/15lb ball</li><li>Standing Lunge – 2x6</li><li>RDL – 2x6</li></ul>

Tuesday	Friday
REST	REST

The Horizontal Jumps

3 WEEK SPECIAL/ TECHNICAL PREPARATION EUROPEAN INFLUENCE

WEEK 1

Sunday	Wednesday
• 10 min easy jog warm up • Static flex, Sprint drills • Short approach jumps – 4-6x 13 strides • Depth jumps – 2x5 (60cm) • S/L Depth – 2x3 (30cm) • 4 stride 4BJ – x4	• Short warm up, Sprint drills • Dynamic flex • Short approach jumps – 4x9 strides • Hurdle hops – 4x5 hurdles • Speed bounding - 4x20m • Med ball THROW – 2x6 each

Monday	Thursday
• Short warm up, Static Flex • Sprint drills, Dynamic flex • 2x (30,40,50,60m) w/ full rec • Hurdle drills – 2x6x6 • Core stability HOLD – 2x30 sec • Postural Series A – 2x15	• Short warm up, Static Flex A, • Sprint drills A, Dynamic flex A • Full approaches – x6 • SFS – 20-20-20 x4 • Hurdle drills – 2x6x6 • Core stability – REP – 2x 20 rep • Postural Series B – 2x15

Tuesday	Friday
• Power Clean – 3x3, 3x2 @85% • ½ box squats – 4x3 @80% slow • Bulgarian SS – 3x8 @20% explosive • Kippin pull ups – 3x8 • Step up – 2x5 (build up) • S/L Hip Extension - 2x8 el	• Split clean – 3x4 @70% • Hang Clean – 3x4 @60% • ½ squats – 3x5 @80% + • Jump split squats – 3x6 el @BW • S/A Cable Rows – 3x8 • RDL – 3x5

WEEK 2

Sunday	Wednesday
<ul><li>10 min easy jog warm up</li><li>Static flex, Sprint drills</li><li>Short approach jumps – 11,13,11,13,11</li><li>Depth jumps – 2x5 (60cm)</li><li>S/L Depth – 2x3 (30cm)</li><li>4 stride 4BJ – x3</li></ul>	<ul><li>Short warm up, Sprint drills</li><li>Dynamic flex</li><li>Short approach jumps – 4x9 strides</li><li>Hurdle hops – 3x5 hurdles</li><li>Speed bounding – 4x20m</li><li>Med ball THROW – 2x6 each</li></ul>

Monday	Thursday
<ul><li>Short warm up, Static Flex</li><li>Sprint drills, Dynamic flex</li><li>2x (30,40,50,60m) w/ full rec</li><li>Hurdle drills – 2x6x6</li><li>Core stability HOLD – 2x30 sec</li><li>Postural Series A – 2x15</li></ul>	<ul><li>Short warm up, Static Flex</li><li>Sprint drills, Dynamic flex</li><li>Full approaches – x4</li><li>SFS – 30-20-30 – x3</li><li>Hurdle drills – 2x6x6</li><li>Core stability REP – 2x20 rep</li><li>Postural Series B – 2x15</li></ul>

Tuesday	Friday
<ul><li>Power Clean – 2x3, 3x2 @87.5%</li><li>½ box squats – 3x3 @80% slow</li><li>Bulgarian SS – 3x8 @20% explosive</li><li>Kippin pull ups – 3x8</li><li>Step up – 2x5 (build up)</li><li>S/L Hip Thruster – 2x8 el</li></ul>	<ul><li>Split Hang clean – 2x4 @70%</li><li>Hang Clean – 2x4@60%</li><li>1/2 squats – 2x5 @80%</li></ul>+<ul><li>Jump split squats – 2x6 el @BW</li><li>S/A Cable rows – 3x8</li><li>RDL – 2x5</li></ul>

WEEK 3

Sunday	Wednesday
<ul><li>10 min easy jog warm up</li><li>Static flex B, Sprint drills B</li><li>13 stride LJ TEST:</li><li>Max 4BJ TEST:</li></ul>	REST

Monday	Thursday
REST	<ul><li>10 min easy jog warm up</li><li>Static flex B, Sprint drills B</li><li>40m Sprint TEST:</li><li>12m-1m Approach TEST:</li></ul> Weights:<ul><li>Power Clean TEST:</li><li>Max Vertical jump TEST:</li><li>RDL – 2x5</li><li>Postural Series B – 2x15</li></ul>

Tuesday	Friday
<ul><li>Short warm up, static flex</li><li>Sprint drills, dynamic flex</li><li>5x30m sprints</li></ul> Weights:<ul><li>Power Clean – 4x3 @80%</li><li>Squat TEST:</li><li>Kippin pull up – 2x8</li><li>Step up – 3x5</li><li>S/L Hip Thruster – 2x8 el</li></ul>	REST

The Horizontal Jumps

EXAMPLE OF EARLY SEASON COMPETITION WEEK EUROPEAN INFLUENCE

Sunday	Thursday
<ul><li>Slow warm up, Dynamic flex, sprint drills</li><li>Short approach jumps – 6x11 strides</li><li>2 stride 4BJ – x4</li><li>Med ball circuit – 2x 6 reps</li><li>Core stability – Hold – 2x30 sec</li></ul>	<ul><li>Short warm up, static flex</li><li>Sprint drills, dynamic flex</li><li>5x30m sprints</li><li>9 stride LJ – x3</li></ul>
Monday	Friday
<ul><li>Short warm up, static flex</li><li>Sprint drills, dynamic flex</li><li>Full approaches – x4-6</li><li>60m sprints – x2</li></ul>	<ul><li>Short warm up, static flex</li><li>Sprint drills, dynamic flex</li><li>5x30m strides</li></ul>
Tuesday	Saturday
<ul><li>Power Cleans – 6x3 (3@80%) FAST</li><li>Jump squats – 4x5 @30% FAST</li><li>Kippin pull ups – 2x6</li><li>Dynamic step ups – 2x6 @20% FAST</li></ul>	<ul><li>Competition</li></ul>

The Horizontal Jumps

EXAMPLE OF MAIN SEASON COMPETITION WEEK
EUROPEAN INFLUENCE

Sunday	Thursday
• Slow warm up, Dynamic flex, sprint drills • Short approach jumps – 6x11 strides • Med ball circuit – 2x 6 reps • Core stability – Hold – 2x30 sec	• Short warm up, static flex • Sprint drills, dynamic flex • 4x10, 3x20, 2x30m sprints • 9 stride LJ – x3

Monday	Friday
• REST	• Short warm up, static flex • Sprint drills, dynamic flex • 5x30m strides

Tuesday	Saturday
• Short warm up, static flex • Sprint drills, dynamic flex • Full approaches – x4 • 60m sprints – x2 • 4BJ – x2 w/4 run in strides Weights PM) • Split Power Cleans – 4x2 @80% FAST • Jump squats – 4x5 @30% FAST • Kippin pull ups – 2x6 • Dynamic step up – 2x6 @20%FAST	• Competition

The Horizontal Jumps

EXAMPLE OF PEAK COMPETITION WEEK
EUROPEAN INFLUENCE

Sunday	Thursday
• REST	• Short warm up, static flex • Sprint drills, dynamic flex • 4x10, 3x20, 2x30m sprints • 11 stride LJ – x2

Monday	Friday
• Short warm up, static flex • Sprint drills, dynamic flex • Full approaches – x4 • 60m sprints – x2 • 4BJ – x2 w/4 run in strides Weights PM) • Split Power Cleans – 4x2 @80% FAST • Jump squats – 4x5 @30% FAST • Kippin pull ups – 2x6 • Dynamic step ups – 2x6 @20% FAST	• Short warm up, static flex • Sprint drills, dynamic flex • 5x30m strides

Wednesday	Saturday
• Short warm up, static flex • Sprint drills, dynamic flex • 5x50m strides	• Competition

Several other set-up options include:

OPTION 1

Mon – Speed / Plyos / Med ball

Tues – REST

Wed – Speed / Weights

Thurs – Technical Session / Plyos

Fri – REST

Sat – Speed / Weights

Sun – REST

OPTION 2

Mon – Speed / Weights

Tues – Plyos / Med ball

Wed – REST

Thurs – Technical Session / Plyos

Fri – Speed

Sat – Weights

Sun – REST

OPTION 3

Mon – Plyos

Tues – Speed / Weights

Wed – REST

Thurs – Technical Session / Plyos

Fri – Speed / Weights

Sat – Speed En / Tempo / Circuits / Med ball

Sun – REST

OPTION 4

Mon – Speed / Plyos

Tues – Weights

Wed – REST

Thurs – Technical Session / Plyos

Fri – Speed

Sat – Weights

Sun – REST

8

SPECIAL EXERCISE PICTURES AND DESCRIPTIONS

A closer look at some specific exercises used within the training program of horizontal jumpers. Includes step by step pictures, descriptions and a full exercise inventory

Nick Newman
The Horizontal Jumps: Planning for Long Term Development

CHAPTER 8

SPECIAL EXERCISE PICTURES AND DESCRIPTIONS

PLYOMETRIC EXERCISES

Beginner & Intermediate Plyometric Exercises

1. Single leg hopping
2. Variation hopping
3. Two foot ankle hops (B)
4. Forward and backward Skipping (B)
5. Standing vertical jumps (B)
6. Standing Long Jump
7. Forward box drop (B)
8. Alternate step up jumps (I)
9. Forward barrier hops (I)

SINGLE LEG HOP

These are very low intensity jumps performed in a continuous fashion either standing in place or while moving forward, backward or in a lateral direction.

Focus should be placed on keeping the free leg in the knee drive position (as in during the long jump takeoff – hip flexed, knee flexed, ankle dorsi flexed).

Focus for the support leg should be on maintaining a heel-toe contact during each hop.

The Horizontal Jumps

VARIATION BOUNDING

These are performed the same way as Single Leg Hopping but this time you will alternate between left (L) and right (R) foot. Different variations can be performed. Variations such as LLRR or LLRRRLLLR, etc., require coordination, postural control and rhythm which can aid in the development of all kinds of sprinting and jumping. These low intensity plyometric movements teach the correct movement patterns needed for take-off while assistive muscles needed during higher intensity sprinting and jumping.

TWO FOOT ANKLE HOPS

This exercise is performed with the person standing on both feet and jumping continuously up and down with as little knee bend as possible.

It is important to keep stiff legs throughout the exercises and not to let the heels contact the ground. This promotes leg stiffness needed during take-off and helps to develop quickness and reactive power of the ankle support system.

The Horizontal Jumps

FORWARD SKIPPING

This is a single leg exercise that can be performed at high or low intensity depending on the goal for that session. It can be performed from a standing or running start and for height or distance.

The action requires a single leg start, pushing off that leg and jumping up and forward in a continuous manner, alternating jump leg each time. Focus is placed on the knee drive of the free leg and the full extension of the support leg.

STANDING VERTICAL JUMP

This exercise is similar to the ankle hops. However, this is developing total leg power by targeting the ankles, knees and hip muscle groups. The exercise is performed by standing on both feet in an upright stance. Quickly lower your hips by bending at the knee and then rapidly jump as high as you can. The speed of movement is the key to this exercise. A quick and powerful change of direction from down to up is an essential part of high level jumping. Arms are used in sequence to aid the jump or can be placed on the hips throughout the movement.

The Horizontal Jumps

STANDING LONG JUMP

The standing long jump is very similar to the vertical jump. It develops leg power and can also be used to practice long jump landings when performed into the sand pit.

HURDLE JUMPS/HOPS

This exercise can be performed at both a high and low intensity. An early progression can be performed over low barriers with a slight pause in between each jump. These are called *hurdle jumps*. An advanced progression will include higher barriers while performing continuous jumps with as minimal ground contact time as possible. Heels should not touch the floor during the advanced progression. These are called *hurdle hops*.

Advanced Plyometric Exercises

1. Alternate Bounding
2. Standing Triple Jump
3. Single Leg Bounding
4. Depth Jumps
5. Continuous Depth Jumps
6. Single Leg Depth Jumps

ALTERNATE BOUNDING

Alternate bounding is a staple exercise for horizontal jumpers. It develops strength, power, technique and control very specific to the demands of the event.

Basically speaking, this exercise requires the athlete to jump forward from one leg to another in a continuous action. To increase the intensity of the exercise, running strides are added before the first bound.

A very advanced method is to have the athlete sprint all out for 20-30m prior to bounding. This takes great strength and confidence to perform.

As bounding is generally a very important exercise in the training program, it is important to describe the key technical requirements of the skill. Listed below are the important elements required during all types of bounding exercises.

1. Maintain upright control of the upper body.
2. Drive arms and free leg forward and upwards during ground strike.
3. Ground strike should be slightly ahead of the hips with a flat foot.
4. Actively drive the support leg backward upon ground strike, strike foot should swing back toward the butt.
5. Maintain rigid support leg during ground strike.

The Horizontal Jumps

STANDING TRIPLE JUMP

This exercise takes great coordination, skill and strength and is very specific for a horizontal jumper. Long and triple jumpers will perform this as part of their training routine and often during testing sessions. It consists of a hop phase, a step phase and a jump phase, no different than the triple jump event itself. The athlete will start with both feet next to each other and then jump forward onto his left leg, and again jump forward on to his right leg and then finally jumping into sand performing a normal landing.

SINGLE LEG BOUNDING

This exercise is very high intensity and consists of the athlete continuously jumping on one leg in a forward direction. An advanced progression of this exercise is to sprint for 10-20m and then begin single leg jumping. Unlike with single leg hopping, here the athlete is aiming for maximal distance with each jump.

When performed correctly the support leg drives down and back into the ground while the free leg drives upwards and forward to complete the action.

DEPTH JUMPS

This exercise should be used by subjects who have mastered the previous exercises and who have a high relative strength base. Athletes stand on a box (30-90cm) and drop to floor (do not jump down).

The athlete's leg muscles want to remain relaxed prior to ground contact. Upon contact with a flat foot the athlete immediately jumps back up as high and as fast as possible.

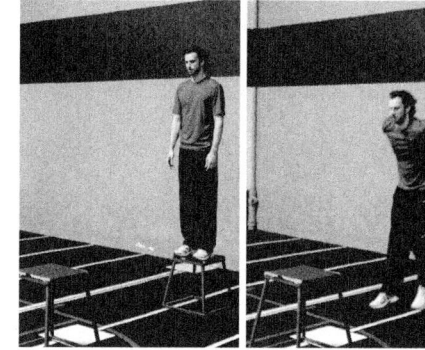

The Horizontal Jumps

SPECIAL WEIGHT TRAINING EXERCISES

1. SPLIT POWER / HANG CLEAN

Description: Start in a squat position while gripping the bar with hands shoulder width apart. Arms are locked, and back arch is very strong with shoulders pulled back. While holding breath the lifter maintains strong back arch and lifts the bar from the floor. The legs and lower back are mainly responsible for this first movement (first pull). The bar should be steadily accelerated from the floor until the lifters ankles, knees, and hips are fully extended and shoulders are in a full shrug position (second pull). As momentum causes the bar to rise to its highest point the lifter will rapidly flip the wrists and drop under the bar catching it on his/her front shoulders. At the same time the lifter will perform a split squat. The split squat and the bar catch are to be performed and completed at the same time.

Notes: To perform the Hang version of this exercise simply start by holding the bar at mid thigh/hip level in a standing position. Perform a slight but rapid drop followed by the second pull and catch as detailed above.

2. SPLIT POWER / HANG SNATCH

Description: Start in a squat position while gripping the bar with hands twice shoulder-width apart. Arms are locked, and back arch is very strong with shoulders pulled back. While holding breath the lifter maintains strong back arch and lifts the bar from the floor. The legs and lower back are mainly responsible for this first movement (first pull). The bar should be steadily accelerated from the floor until the lifters ankles, knees, and hips are fully extended and shoulders are in a full shrug position (second pull). As momentum causes the bar to rise to its highest point the lifter will rapidly flip the wrists and drop under the bar catching it high above the head with fully extended and arms. At the same time the lifter will perform a split squat. The split squat and the bar catch are to be performed and completed at the same time

Notes: To perform the Hang version of this exercise simply start by holding the bar at mid thigh/hip level in a standing position. Perform a slight but rapid drop followed by the second pull and catch as detailed above.

3. CONTINUOUS JUMP SQUAT

Description: Start in a regular squat position with bar placed on upper traps and feet shoulder width apart. The lifter will rapidly perform vertical jumps while maintaining starting bar position. All jumps are to be performed in a continuous fashion as fast as possible.

Notes: This exercise is to be performed with stiff/rigid legs and it is vital that the upward speed of the bar is maintained at maximum.

The Horizontal Jumps

4. DROP CATCH JUMP SQUAT

Description: Same starting position as with Continuous Jump Squats. This time however the lifter will rapidly drop into a parallel squat position and immediately react and jump up as high as possible. After each repetition is performed a pause/reset of 1-2 seconds will be performed.

Notes: The key to this exercise is the speed at which the bar is stopped from the downward motion and changes to an upward motion.

5. QUARTER SQUAT

Description: Same as regular squat but the downward movement is limited to only a slight knee bend.

Notes: The lifter will be able to handle considerably higher loads with this squat action than with a deep or parallel squat. Therefore, maintaining correct back position with a strong back arch throughout the movement is very important.

6. SINGLE LEG SQUAT / BULGARIAN SPLIT SQUAT

Description: Could also be called a *Reaction Bulgarian Split Squat*. Here, the starting position has one leg placed on a support behind front leg with dumbbells held in each hand. The lifter will rapidly drive upwards on the front leg and perform continuous jumps.

Notes: During any dynamic single leg exercise it is vital that a strong lower back position and core is maintained throughout. Relaxation of the core muscles could cause injury to the SI joint and/or lower back.

7. SPLIT JUMP

Description: The lifter will start in a standing position with bar placed on upper traps or with dumbbells in each hand. The feet will be placed in a staggered position with one foot slightly in front of the other. The lifter will jump in a continuous fashion maintaining stiff/rigid legs throughout. Rapidly after each jump is performed the front and back foot will switch ready for landing and the following jump.

The Horizontal Jumps

8. DYNAMIC STEP UP

Description: The lifter will start in a standing position with bar placed on upper traps or with dumbbells in each hand and with one foot in front up on a box. The lifter will rapidly drive upwards onto the box until support leg is fully extended. Each repetition will be performed with an upward and downward movement of the same leg. When the non support leg touches the floor the lifter immediately drives back up on the box.

Notes: Each set will be performed one leg at a time. This will allow the lifter to perform each repetition as fast as possible.

9. SINGLE LEG ROMANIAN DEADLIFT (RDL)

Description: To perform a left leg RDL the lifter starts in a standing position with a dumbbell held in the right hand. Throughout the movement the support leg (left leg) will be slightly bent and the back/core will remain strong/solid. The lifter will begin lowering the dumbbell by flexing the left hip and extending the right hip. Back arch is to be maintained throughout the movement.

Notes: When a stretch in the support leg is felt in the hamstring the lifter will begin returning the start position and the repetition is complete.

10. SINGLE LEG HIP THRUSTER

Description: Starting in a supine position with knees bent and the flats of both feet planted on the floor the lifter will extend one leg and raise the hips using the force of the support leg

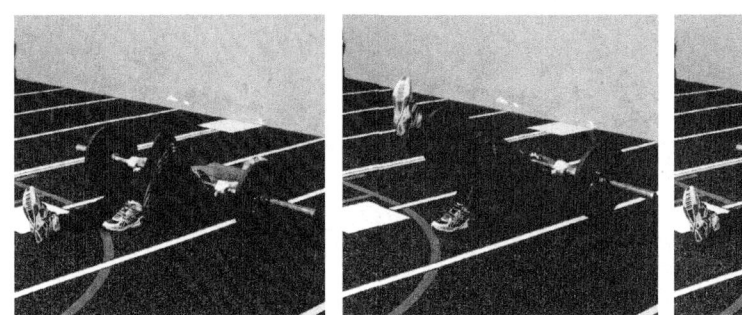

Notes: Maintain a strong/solid core to avoid the dropping of the non-support leg side and hip.

11. BACK EXTENSION W/MB RAISE

Description: Regular starting position in back extension machine. Perform extension while holding a medicine ball above the head.

The Horizontal Jumps

Notes: Do not over-extend at the finish of the upward movement. The upward movement is complete once torso is parallel to the floor.

12.   HANGING LEG RAISES

Description: Starting in a regular overhand grip pull up position the lifter will raise both straight legs together to a parallel position. Slowly lower and repeat movement.

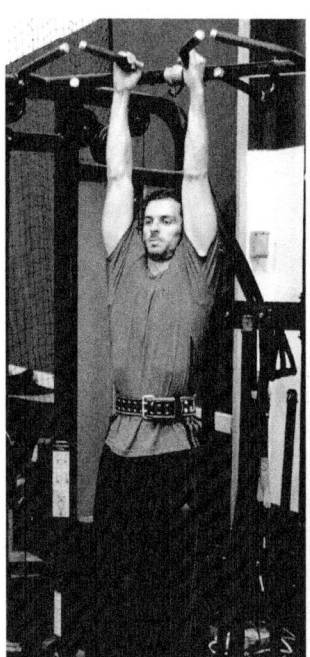

Notes: There are many variations of this exercise. Advanced athletes may be able to raise straight legs to a vertical position while beginner athletes may start with knee raises or alternate knee raise instead.

MEDICINE BALL EXERCISES

VERTICAL THROW

OVERHEAD FORWARD

OVERHEAD BACKWARD

BETWEEN THE LEGS FORWARD

The Horizontal Jumps

TRAINING INVENTORY EXERCISE DESCRIPTIONS

STATIC FLEX A

Knees to Chest – *Lying on the floor while pulling one knee toward the chest*
Single Hamstring – *Lying on the floor while holding one leg straight in a vertical position*
Seated Quad – *While seated lean back with one leg bent and with foot under bottom*
Front Lunge Glute – *In lunge position lean forward placing inside foreman level with front heel*
Front Lunge Hip – *In lunge position with upright torso push hips forward*
Adductor Hamstring Rotation – *On one knee with straight leg in front, rotate torso away*
Standing IT Band Stretch – *Cross one leg far behind other, bend torso toward back foot*

STATIC FLEX B

DEEP Squat – *Regular squat position sitting as low as possible*
Hurdle Stretch – *Seated on ground in exact position as when hurdling*
Seated Plough – *Same position as hurdle stretch but front leg in bent and turned inwards*
Butterfly – *Seated position with bent legs, feet together and knees pointed outwards*
Heel Sits – *Sit on heels and lean back with hands on the ground*
Toe Touch – *Same as hurdle stretch but with bent leg* turned inward instead of outward
Calf Stretch – *Downward dog position with instep of one foot on the heel of the other*

SPRINT DRILLS A

Walking A Skip – *Walking with parallel knee lift on each step*
Walking B Skip – *Walking with parallel knee lift followed my knee extension on each step*

A Skip – *Rhythmic forward hops with alternate parallel knee lift*
B Skip – *Same as A skip but each parallel knee lift is followed with a knee extension*
Ankling – *Similar to fast walking with fast ankle movements while staying in ground contact*
High Knees – *Bouncy running with excessive high knee action during each stride*
Butt Kickers – *Bouncy running with low knee lift and excessive backside kicking*
Backward Run – *Normal running but backward with a forward lean*

SPRINT DRILLS B

Straight Leg Bounds – *Regular running while keeping leg straight*
Alt Fast Legs – *Forward jogging with irregular alternate fast strides*
Alt Double Butt Kickers – *Same as butt kickers but with two consecutive on each leg*
Side Skips – *Moving laterally while skipping*
Carioca's – *Moving laterally while alternating forward and back leg crossovers*

DYNAMIC FLEX A

Hip Circle – *Standing while moving waste in circular motion*
Trunk Rotation – *Standing while rotating waste clockwise and anti-clockwise*
Knee Drives – *Standing while swinging bent leg forward and backward*
Front Leg Swings – *Standing while swinging straight leg forward and backward*
Side Leg Swings – *Standing while swinging straight leg medially and laterally*
Seated Quads – *Same as seated quad but with forward hip thrusting action*
Scissor Kicks – *Laying with legs vertical while crossing forward/backward or medial/lateral*
Alt Hurdle stretch – *Same as hurdle stretch but with alternating left/right leg switch*

DYNAMIC FLEX B

Walking Knee Grab – *Walking with alternate knee pull toward chest*
Straight Leg Kicks – *Walking with alternate straight leg high kicks*
Walking Twist Lunges – *Walking lunge with torso rotation*
Exaggerated Knee Runs – *Normal running with extra excessive high knee action*

HURDLE DRILLS A

Forward Step Over – *Stepping over hurdles with same lead leg*
Forward Alt Step Over – *Stepping over hurdle with alternating lead leg*
Side Step Over – *Stepping over hurdles laterally*
Backward Step Over – *Backward stepping over hurdles with alternating lead leg*
Side Kicks – *Continuous straight leg lateral kicks over hurdles*
Over and Under – *Forward step over followed by forward step under the hurdle*

HURDLE DRILLS B

A Skips – *Regular A skip but in rhythm over hurdles*
B Skips - *Regular B skip but in rhythm over hurdles*
Skip Over – *Regular skipping action in rhythm over hurdles*

The Horizontal Jumps

GENERAL STRENGTH

SQUAT WALK SERIES

Forward Squat Walk – *Deep squat position while walking forward*
Lateral Squat Walk – *Deep squat position while walking laterally*
Squat w/Kick – *Same as squat walk but with knee extension during each step*
Backward Squat Walk – *Same as squat walk but backward*

LUNGE SERIES

Standing Front Lunge – *Forward lunge returning back to start position*
Side Lunge – *Lateral lunge returning to start position*
Standing Backward Lunge – *Reverse lunge returning forward to start position*
Walking Lunge w/Twist - *Continuous forward lunges with torso rotation*
Low Walking Lunge – *Deep squat position continuous forward lunges*

ANKLE SERIES

Bunny Hops – *Low intensity jumping while moving forward*
Zig Zag Hops – *Low intensity jumping from left to right while moving forward*
Side Hops – *Low intensity jumping while moving laterally*
Forward/Backward Hops – *Low intensity jumping moving forward and backward*
Standing Single Leg Hops – *Low intensity vertical jumps on one leg*

POSTURAL SERIES A

Squat – *Regular body weight squat to parallel*
Core hold w/Knee raise – *Supine, stomach tight, back flat w/alt knee knees*
S/L Squat – *Regular single leg squat w/free leg behind*
Core hold w/leg ext – *Supine, stomach tight, back flat w/knees bent, alt leg ext*
Side step down – *S/L squat on box w/free leg straight. Lower until knee touches floor*

Core hold w/leg raise – *Supine, stomach tight, back flat w/straight legs, alt leg raise*
Lunge w/rotation – *Forward lunge w/core rotation toward forward knee*
All 4 w/alt arm/leg etc – *All 4 position, raise alt arm and leg*
S/L squat & reach – *S/L squat w/opposite arm reach and touch cone*

POSTURAL SERIES B

Overhead Squat – *Regular snatch grip overhead squat to parallel*
Side bridge w/hip abduction – *Side bridge w/top leg raise*
Assisted S/L Squat – *S/L squat w/opposite hard holding TRX/Band*
Core hold w/doubt leg ext – *Supine, stomach tight, back flat, knees up w/double leg extension*
Dynamic step up – *Fast continuous step ups*
Quad Rocker – *All 4 position, slowly rock back and forward keeping back straight*
Side Lunge – *Regular side lunge*
All 4 w/external hip rotation – *All 4 position, externally rotate alt hips*
S/L hop & stick – *S/L forward hop w/2 second pause on landing*

CORE SERIES

MB crunch w/alt knee tap – *Regular crunch with medicine ball alternating knee touches*
MB full sit-up – *Crunch position from lying down to fully sitting up with a medicine ball in hand*
MB superman – *Regular superman raising medicine ball off the ground above head*
Crunch & Spin – *Regular crunch followed by 180 degree spin keeping chest and feet up*
Straight leg raise – *Supine position raising leg up while keeping low back flat*
Alt superman – *Prone position alternating left/right arm/leg raises*

ADVANCED CORE SERIES

SB Crunch w/weight – *Regular crunch lying on stability ball holding dumbbell*
- **SB Glute bridge pull over** – *Upper shoulders resting on stability ball in glute bridge position while performing straight arm chest pull over with dumbbell*
- **SB Crunch** – *Regular crunch while lying on stability ball*

Straight leg oblique crunch – *Regular crunch while lying on side and raising both legs together*
- **SB side bridge** – *Regular side bridge position with foreman resting on stability ball*

SB push up bridge leg raise series – *Pushup position with hands on stability, alternating forward and side knee drives*
- **Same w/feet on bench** – *As above but with hands on stability ball and feet on bench*

Back hyper w/MB raise – *On back extension machine, perform back extension with shoulder raise holding medicine ball*

Hanging knee raise w/MB hit – *Hang in pull up position while raising both knees, have partner hit medicine ball against stomach*

MED BALL CIRCUIT A

Sit up w/throw – *Regular sit up with medicine ball overhead throw forward*
Hyper w/throw – *Regular superman with medicine ball throw forward*
½ squat holding ball out – *Regular ½ squat while holding medicine ball straight out in front*
Seated horizontal kick flicks – *Seated with medicine ball between feet, drive ball upwards*
Lunge holding ball out – *Regular forward lunge while holding medicine ball out in front*
Supine kick w/catch & crunch – *Lay flat with ball between feet, drive upwards and catch into regular crunch*
Side to side hyper – *Using back extension machine lie sideward for side raises while holding medicine ball*
Standing kick flicks w/catch – *Stand with medicine ball between feet, jump and drive ball upwards and catch*

Vertical slams – *Stand with ball straight above head, slam down in front with straight arms*

5 Bunny hops holding ball out – *Holding medicine ball straight out in front perform 5 bunny hops*

MED BALL CIRCUIT B

Sit up throw – *Regular sit and forward throw*

Superman throw – *Regular superman and forward throw*

BL Vertical throw – *Holding medicine ball squat with ball between legs and throw vertically*

Russian twist throw – *Holding medicine ball in seated position twist and throw*

Standing twist throw – *Standing facing the wall holding medicine ball twist and throw forward*

Vertical chest throw – *Holding medicine ball in chest pass position, squat and jump throwing ball vertically*

Side slams – *Holding medicine ball straight above head, alternating downward slams each side of the body*

Front slams - *Stand with ball straight above head, slam down in front with straight arms*

BL Backward throw – *Holding medicine ball squat with ball between legs and throw overhead backward*

MULTI JUMP CIRCUITS

HOPPING A

LLL/RRR – *Low intensity linear hopping on one leg, free leg remains with parallel thigh*
LRLR – *Same as above alternating from left to right leg*
RRLL/LLRR – *Same as above in a left, left, right, right pattern*

HOPPING B

Medial (L&R) – *Same as above moving in medial direction (Right leg moving toward left)*
Lateral (L&R) – *Same as above moving in lateral direction (Left leg moving toward left)*
S/L For/Back hops (L&R) – *Same as above moving in forward and backward direction*
Zig Zag hops (L&R) – *Same as above moving forward in zig zag pattern*

ENDURANCE BOUNDING A

LLL > 30m – *Single leg continuous jumping on same leg for distance*
RRR > 30m – *Same as above*
LRLR > 50m – *Alternate continuous jumping from one leg to the other for distance*
LLRR > 50m – *Same as above*

ENDURANCE BOUNDING B

Power Skips > 60m – *Regular skipping for height/distance using double swing*
Continuous Takeoffs > 40m – *Continuous long jump takeoffs with 2-3 running strides in between*
Backward Skips > 60m – *Regular skipping for height/distance moving backward*

SPECIFIC BOUNDING A

Standing long jump – *2 foot explosive jump for horizontal distance*
5 Frog jumps – *5 consecutive standing long jumps for distance*
5 bounds – *5 consecutive alternate bounds for distance*
5 Hops (L&R) – *5 consecutive single leg bounds for distance*

SPECIFIC BOUNDING B

Vertical hops – *Low intensity vertical jumps with minimal knee bend*
Single leg vertical hops – *As above but on one leg*
Tuck jumps – *Vertical jumps while driving both knees to chest*
Split jumps – *Vertical jumps while performing side split action*
Pike jumps – *Vertical jumps while driving legs forward and touching toes*

SPECIFIC BOUNDING C

Bench jumps – *Start sitting on a low bench and perform vertical jump*
S/L hops – *Low intensity vertical jumps on one leg*
Wide out freeze – *Vertical jump landing in a wide squat with minimal eccentric movement*
S/L Bench jumps – *Same a regular bench jumps but using one leg*
Side to side – *Low intensity jumps from side to side*
S/L figure 8 – *Multiple jumps performed in a figure 8 pattern*

BOX JUMP A

2 foot depth jump (Ball of foot) – *Drop off box and with no heel ground contact immediately perform vertical jump*
2 foot depth jump (Flat foot) - *As above but landing on a flat foot*

BOX JUMP B

1 foot depth jump (Height) – *As regular (flat foot) depth jump but on one leg for height*
1 foot depth jump (Distance) – *As above but performed for distance*
1 foot depth jump (Sand landing) – *As above but finish landing in sand pit*

THROWING POWER

MED BALL THROW A

Soccer Throw – *Regular soccer style throw in with a medicine ball*
BTL backward - *Holding medicine ball squat with ball between legs and throw overhead backward*
BTL vertical – *As above but throw ball vertically*
BTL forward – *As above but throw ball forward*
Side Throws - *Standing twist and throw sideward*

MED BALL THROW B

Running D/L Soccer Throw – *Regular soccer style throw in using a running start*
Running DL Chest pass – *Regular chest pass using a running start*
Running S/L Soccer Throw – *Regular soccer style throw in off one leg using a running start*
Running S/L Chest pass – *Regular chest pass off one leg using a running start*

WEIGHT CIRCUIT

TOTAL BODY LONG A

SB Glute bridge w/alt knee ext – *Glute Bridge with upper shoulders on ball while alternating knee extension*
Lateral raise – *Standing lateral shoulder raises*
Decline pushups - *Pushups performed with feet raised on bench*
Close supine pull ups – *Pull ups performed under fixed bar in supine position*
DB bicep curls – *Regular bicep curls performed with dumbbells*
SL Hip thrusters – *Lying supine position with one leg bent and thrusting hips up*
Prone SB plank w/PU + hip ext – *Feet on stability ball in pushup position, perform pushup while alternating leg raises (hip extension)*
Wide supine pull ups – *As close supine pull ups but with wide grip*
Side hip raises – *Lying on side raising hips up and down*
SB Hamstring curls – *Lying in supine position with feet on stability ball, raise hips and perform knee flexor pulling ball toward you*
Chest flies – *Regular chest flies using dumbbells*
Back ext – *Regular back extension using machine*
BB Bicep curls – *Regular bicep curls using barbell*
Hanging Leg raises – *In pull up position raise both legs up while keeping them straight*
Incline pushups – *Regular pushups performed on a bench with feet on the floor*

CORE STABILITY

REP/HOLD SERIES - FLOOR

S/L Glute bridge – *Regular single leg glute bridge performed on the floor*
Plank w/hip ext – *Regular prone position plank with alternating leg raises*
S/L Straight leg glute bridge – *Lying in supine position with hands back and legs straight, raise hips using alternating straight legs*
Side bridge w/hip abduction – *Regular side bridge while raising top leg*
Elevated glute bridge w/knee ext – *Glute bridge with knee extension while upper shoulders are resting on a bench*

REP/HOLD SERIES - BALL

Prone SB plank w/PU + hip ext – *Feet on stability ball in pushup position, perform pushup while alternating leg raises (hip extension)*
Straight leg glute bridge w/alt hip flex – *Lying in supine position with feet on stability ball, raise hips and alternate leg raises*
Side bridge w/hip abduction – *As regular side bridge w/hip abduction but with forearm resting on stability ball*
Elevated glute bridge w/knee ext – *Upper shoulders on stability ball in glute bridge position with alternating knee extensions*
Bridge on hands w/lateral feet rock – *Feet on stability ball in pushup position while feet rock from side to side*

The Horizontal Jumps

HIP STRENGTH

HANGING ABS

Bent Knee raises – *In pull up position raise both knees to chest*
Alt knee splits – *In pull up position alternate single leg knee raises to chest*
S/L straight leg drives – *In pull up position alternate straight leg raises to parallel*
Straight leg drives – *As above but with both legs at the same time*
Fast Hitch kicks – *In pull up position perform slow hitch kick movements*

HIP SERIES

Supine S/L knee drive – *Lying on a bench perform single leg vertical knee drives*
Prone S/L donkey kick – *Lying in prone position perform single leg vertical heel drives*
Side hip abduction – *Lying on side perform top leg side leg raises*
Side hip adduction – *Lying on side perform bottom leg side raises*
Incline S/L knee drive – *Lying on an incline bench perform single leg vertical knee drives*
Incline S/L donkey kick – *Lying in prone position on an incline bench perform single leg vertical heel drives*

The Horizontal Jumps

JUMPING EVENTS – EXERCISE INVENTORY

WARM-UP

STATIC FLEX A
- ☐ Knees to Chest
- ☐ Single Hamstring
- ☐ Seated Quad
- ☐ Front Lunge Glute
- ☐ Front Lunge Hip
- ☐ Adductor Hamstring Rotation
- ☐ Standing IT Band Stretch

STATIC FLEX B
- ☐ DEEP Squat
- ☐ Hurdle Stretch
- ☐ Seated Plough
- ☐ Butterfly
- ☐ Heel Sits
- ☐ Toe Touch
- ☐ Calf Stretch

SPRINT DRILLS A
- ☐ Walking A Skip
- ☐ Walking B Skip
- ☐ A Skip
- ☐ B Skip
- ☐ Ankling
- ☐ High Knees
- ☐ Butt Kickers
- ☐ Backward Run

SPRINT DRILLS B
- ☐ Straight Leg Bounds
- ☐ Alt Fast Legs
- ☐ Alt Double Butt Kickers
- ☐ Side Skips
- ☐ Carioca's

DYNAMIC FLEX A
- ☐ Hip Circle
- ☐ Trunk Rotation
- ☐ Knee Drives
- ☐ Front Leg Swings
- ☐ Side Leg Swings
- ☐ Seated Quads
- ☐ Scissor Kicks
- ☐ Alt Hurdle stretch

DYNAMIC FLEX B
- ☐ Walking Knee Grab
- ☐ Straight Leg Kicks
- ☐ Walking Twist Lunges
- ☐ Exaggerated Knee Runs

HURDLE DRILLS A
- ☐ Forward Step Over
- ☐ Forward Alt Step Over
- ☐ Side Step Over
- ☐ Backward Step Over
- ☐ Side Kicks
- ☐ Over and Under

HURDLE DRILLS B
- ☐ A Skips
- ☐ B Skips
- ☐ C Skips
- ☐ Skip Over

GENERAL STRENGTH

SQUAT WALK SERIES
- ☐ Forward Squat Walk
- ☐ Lateral Squat Walk
- ☐ Squat w/Kick
- ☐ Backward Squat Walk

LUNGE SERIES
- ☐ Standing Front Lunge
- ☐ Side Lunge
- ☐ Stand Backward Lunge
- ☐ Walking Lunge w/Twist
- ☐ Low Walking Lunge

ANKLE SERIES
- ☐ Bunny Hops
- ☐ Zig Zag Hops
- ☐ Side Hops
- ☐ Forward/Backward Hops
- ☐ Standing Single Leg Hops

POSTURAL SERIES A
- ☐ Squat
- ☐ Core hold w/knee raise
- ☐ S/L Squat
- ☐ Core hold w/leg ext
- ☐ Side step down
- ☐ Core hold w/straight leg raise
- ☐ Lunge w/rotation
- ☐ All 4 w/alt arm/leg ext
- ☐ S/L squat & reach

POSTURAL SERIES B
- ☐ Overhead Squat
- ☐ Side bridge w/hip abduction
- ☐ Assisted S/L squat
- ☐ Core hold w/double leg ext
- ☐ Dynamic step up
- ☐ Quad rocker
- ☐ Side Lunge
- ☐ All 4 w/Ext hip rotation
- ☐ S/L hop & stick

CORE SERIES
- ☐ MB crunch w/alt knee tap
- ☐ MB full sit up
- ☐ MB superman
- ☐ Crunch & Spin
- ☐ Straight leg raise
- ☐ Alt superman

ADVANCED CORE SERIES
- ☐ SB Crunch w/weight
  - ○ SB Glute bridge pull over
  - ○ SB Crunch
- ☐ Straight leg oblique crunch
  - ○ SB side bridge
- ☐ SB push up bridge leg raise series
  - ○ Same w/feet on bench
- ☐ Back hyper w/MB raise
- ☐ Hanging knee raise w/MB hit

MED BALL CIRCUIT A
- ☐ Sit up w/throw
- ☐ Hyper w/throw
- ☐ ½ squat holding ball out
- ☐ Seated horizontal kick flicks
- ☐ Lunge holding ball out
- ☐ Supine kick w/catch & crunch
- ☐ Side to side hyper
- ☐ Standing kick flicks w/catch
- ☐ Vertical slams
- ☐ 5 Bunny hops holding ball out

The Horizontal Jumps

MED BALL CIRCUIT B
- ☐ Sit up throw
- ☐ Superman throw
- ☐ BL Vertical throw
- ☐ Russian twist throw
- ☐ Standing twist throw
- ☐ Vertical chest throw
- ☐ Side slams
- ☐ Front slams
- ☐ BL Backward throw

MULTI JUMP CIRCUITS

HOPPING A
- ☐ LLL/RRR
- ☐ LRLR…
- ☐ RRLL/LLRR

HOPPING B
- ☐ Medial (L&R)
- ☐ Lateral (L&R)
- ☐ S/L For/Back hops (L&R)
- ☐ Zig Zag hops (L&R)

ENDURANCE BOUNDING A
- ☐ LLL > 30m
- ☐ RRR > 30m
- ☐ LRLR > 50m
- ☐ LLRR > 50m

ENDURANCE BOUNDING B
- ☐ Power Skips > 60m
- ☐ Continuous Takeoffs > 40m
- ☐ Backward Skips > 60m

SPECIFIC BOUNDING A
- ☐ Standing long jump
- ☐ 5 Frog jumps
- ☐ 5 bounds
- ☐ 5 Hops (L&R)

SPECIFIC BOUNDING B
- ☐ Vertical hops
- ☐ Single leg vertical hops
- ☐ Tuck jumps
- ☐ Split jumps
- ☐ Pike jumps

SPECIFIC BOUNDING C
- ☐ Bench jumps
- ☐ S/L hops
- ☐ Wide out freeze
- ☐ S/L Bench jumps
- ☐ Side to side
- ☐ S/L figure 8

BOX JUMP A
- ☐ 2 foot depth jump (Ball of foot)
- ☐ 2 foot depth jump (Flat foot)

BOX JUMP B
- ☐ 1 foot depth jump (Height)
- ☐ 1 foot depth jump (Distance)
- ☐ 1 foot depth jump (Sand landing)

THROWING POWER

MED BALL THROW A
- ☐ Soccer throw in
- ☐ BTL backward
- ☐ BTL vertical
- ☐ BTL forward
- ☐ Side throws

MED BALL THROW B
- ☐ Running D/L Soccer Throw
- ☐ Running DL Chest pass
- ☐ Running S/L Soccer Throw
- ☐ Running S/L Chest pass

WEIGHT CIRCUIT

TOTAL BODY LONG A
- ☐ SB Glute bridge w/alt knee ext
- ☐ Lateral raise
- ☐ Decline push ups
- ☐ Close supine pull ups
- ☐ DB bicep curls
- ☐ SL Hip thrusters
- ☐ Prone SB bridge w/PU +
- ☐ hip ext
- ☐ Wide supine pull ups
- ☐ Side hip raises
- ☐ SB Hamstring curls
- ☐ Chest flys
- ☐ Back ext
- ☐ BB Bicep curls
- ☐ Hanging Leg raises
- ☐ Incline push ups

CORE STABILITY

REP/HOLD SERIES - FLOOR
- ☐ S/L Glute bridge
- ☐ Plank w/hip ext
- ☐ S/L Straight leg glute bridge
- ☐ Side plank w/hip abduction
- ☐ Elevated glute bridge w/knee ext

REP/HOLD SERIES - BALL
- ☐ Plank on hands w/hip ext
- ☐ Straight leg glute bridge w/alt hip flex
- ☐ Side bridge w/hip abduction
- ☐ Elevated glute bridge w/knee ext
- ☐ Bridge on hands w/lateral feet rock

HIP STRENGTH

HANGING ABS
- ☐ Bent Knee raises
- ☐ Alt knee splits
- ☐ S/L straight leg drives to vertical
- ☐ Straight leg drives to vertical
- ☐ Fast Hitch kicks

HIP SERIES
- ☐ Supine S/L knee drive
- ☐ Prone S/L donkey kick
- ☐ Side hip abduction
- ☐ Side hip adduction
- ☐ Incline S/L knee drive
- ☐ Incline S/L donkey kick

FINAL THOUGHTS

Bringing closure to the book with 101 tips for the horizontal jumps

Nick Newman
The Horizontal Jumps: Planning
for Long Term Development

FINAL THOUGHTS

I sincerely hope everyone this book reaches enjoys reading it as much as I have enjoyed researching and writing it. It was my aim to positively affect lives of readers in some way, no matter how big or small. I wanted to produce a text that was understandable, to the point, and most importantly meaningful to those who view this sport with as much passion as I do.

To the younger readers or to those new to this sport, be patient and embrace every day you can train. Be passionate and love what you do. Be respectful to those before you and those who aim for the same goals you aim for.

Understand that nothing worth working so hard for will come easy and be handed to you on a plate. Demonstrate great perseverance and work not only hard but as smart as you can. Do everything you can do to learn about your body and this sport and do not solely rely on everyone to achieve your goals and dreams for you.

My final words: The world meets nobody halfway. You must do for yourself. You must strive every day, leaving no stone unturned until every option has been exhausted. Never be in a rush and instead enjoy every aspect of the journey. Only then will the destination be as sweet as you envisioned it to be. You can achieve anything your heart and mind desires. Never give up until you are who you wanted to become.

101 GENERAL TIPS FOR THE HORIZONTAL JUMPS

1. Training must be progressive in some way in order for continued adaptation to occur

2. Adaptations are specific. General training will cause general adaptation

3. Many short training phases will allow greater continued development than fewer longer phases

4. General training transitions to specific training over time

5. Intensity is the most important training variable for jumpers

6. Adaptations occur when stress is experienced for a long enough time and at a high enough frequency

7. General mobility and flexibility should be maintained at all times

8. Quality of training far outweighs the importance of quantity of training

9. Sprinting speed is very important but the ability to transition into a takeoff at speed is more important

10. Maximum strength is of huge importance for jumpers

11. Olympic weightlifting exercises should be the basis for strength/power development

12. Bilateral exercises gradually transition toward unilateral exercises

13. Do not be afraid to occasionally rest instead of train. Listen to your mind and body

14. Visual control is of huge importance with regards to legal jumping

15. Convince yourself that it is OK to take off from the back of the takeoff board

16. The most common mistake that does not receive a lot of attention is the ability to land efficiently.

17. Landing efficiently should not be complicated. Dig heels out in front and pull hips through. Let momentum take you

18. Recovery and rest need lots of attention. Away from training do all you can to aid recovery

19. If you can run fast, bound far, clean and squat a lot, and have average or better technique the odds are you can perform well in the horizontal jumps

20. Injury prevention training should be included throughout the entire training year

21. A strong lower back and core will go a long way to prevent injuries

22. Take your time during training sessions. Too much rest is always better than not enough

23. Set yourself training goals for each phase. Write them down and look at them daily

24. Keep stats on your training. Log every single number you can throughout your journey as an athlete and coach

25. Under training can be just as negative as over training

26. Your body should feel considerably different during unload weeks. If the difference is not extremely noticeable you should re-think your unload strategy

27. Speed and power development should be the primary focus on training for jumpers

28. Once extremely high levels of speed and power have been achieved the jumpers fate lies firmly in technique and mental ability

29. The majority of physical adaptations achieved through this type of training will occur within the central nervous system

30. Plyometric training is very important but is often used in too large volumes. Generally 3-4 exercises should be used per session with lots of rest between sets and exercises

31. The ability of the takeoff leg to handle forces and not buckle will largely determine jump distance

32. Training variety is important but deliberate progressions need to be a focus throughout the year

33. Progressions are individual and should be used only when the athlete is ready to progress

34. Increase training intensity rather than training volume

35. In order for a fatigued athlete to perform quality work the overall load must be decreased

36. If you can squat 2.2 times and clean 1.6 times your body weight you are at a very high level with those exercises

37. Maximum strength highly correlates with static jump exercises such as standing bounding, vertical jumping and very short approach long/triple jumps

38. Maximum speed and speed weights highly correlate with long approach long/triple jump and running bounding exercises

39. The more you have of a specific ability related to horizontal jumping performance the less you need of another to perform well

40. If you can only train 3 times per week you should include a technical session with plyometric training, a sprinting session with plyometric training, and a weight training session

41. Keep upper body bulk/size to a minimum. You do not need a big upper body to sprint fast, jump far, or to lift heavy weights

42. After sufficient strength is achieved the focus should switch to the speed at which you can move 50-80% of your maximum

43. Visualize perfect technique on a regular basis. This includes hitting the board legally

44. Find a pair of training sneakers and spikes that you like and always buy the same ones

45. Performing squat exercises while raising your heels an inch or two off the ground can greatly benefit your lower back

46. Be ready to compete. Arrange your training accordingly and do not waste meets on short approach jumps

47. Periodically change your warm-up routine

48. Do not over analyze your technique, training and performance. This will cause more problems than you had before

49. Lay flat with your feet up high against a wall at least 15 minutes a day

50. Find a supplement combination that you like and stick with it. Typically, a creatine source, a protein and amino acid supplement, a pre-training boost and other recovery aid supplements work well

51. Use a custom fit shoe insole that you place in an oven and then mold to your feet and use them in your sneakers and spikes

52. Do not be afraid to enjoy your big foul jumps. Regardless of what others may say this shows your true physical ability and potential

53. Be an athlete 24 hours a day, not just the few hours that you train

54. Include a tape measure, white tape, a stop watch, cones, a drink, and a snack bar in your daily workout bag

55. Training intensity can be higher and recovery times shorter in warm weather. The opposite is true in colder weather

56. If you have done something once you can absolutely do it again

57. Do not focus on others especially when in a competition.

58. Do not chase numbers or focus on outcome goals

59. Record technical training often and compare important technical components over time

60. Do not be afraid to repeat successful training blocks/phases

61. Younger and older athletes should allow more time between high intensity sessions

62. Avoid spending hours at a competition before you are ready to compete. Try to get there 1.5 hours before you are scheduled to jump

63. While traveling to different cities, countries, and hotels for competitions, stay occupied with things other than track and field

64. It is common to perform well after you have had a cold or flu bug

65. Always be confident no matter who you are jumping against

66. Find a routine that works for you and perform it every time you compete

67. Figure out if you are the aggressive jumper or the passive jumper. Aggressive jumpers need to scream and shout, bang their chest and walk around between jumps. Passive jumpers will lie down between jumps and stay quiet. Do not let who you jump against change who you are as a jumper

68. The horizontal jumps will never be performed perfectly

69. Competitive jump sessions against training partners can add a lot of fun to a training session

70. Measuring jumps during technical sessions can give valuable information but can also detract from the technical focus

71. Timing all sprint repetitions gives valuable information with a training session, including improvement, fatigue levels, and consistency

72. Be selective who you take advice from. Often too many people have contradicting advice to give the same athlete

73. Perform a hard training session at least 24 hours before you take a long flight and 24-48 hours after a long flight

74. Rapid improvements in speed for young athletes will likely create takeoff problems in the short term

75. You should aim to hit 95+% of your fastest fly 10m or fly 5m time on the runway

76. It is possible for a male jumper to jump over 8 meters in the long jump and 17 meters in the triple jump running under 10 m/s

77. You will never create the perfect training program. Even for the most scientifically minded coach/athlete this is not an exact science

78. Although difficult, it is possible to increase horizontal velocity during the takeoff action

79. Be prepared to sacrifice many aspects of your life if you truly want to reach the top level in this sport

80. Study the sport and become a student of what you do

81. Very few jumpers have ever been able to effectively land the 2½ hitch kick

82. Injuries are absolutely a part of the sport no matter how well prepared you are

83. Concentration of the highest order is required when on the runway

84. If you foul by an inch and you move back a foot you will likely foul by an inch again.

85. A successful training program is a successful training program no matter if you later learned you made many mistakes or not

86. Base predictions on training achievements. You should compete the way you train

87. If you are going to ask for a clap, ask during your first jump and ask every jump after that

88. Effective sprint technique and an effective takeoff is one that is patiently performed. Do not rush your movement

89. A taller jumper may not become as strong as a short jumper. A taller jumper, however, possesses physical qualities that a shorter jumper will never possess. Know who you are and train accordingly

90. Use a check mark on the runway. Perfect the first phase of the approach run

91. During training make sure the sand is not too hard. Work the pit before you jump

92. If you train with no board, create a white tape board for every technical session

93. During technical sessions if you are struggling to execute from a certain stride number, be sure to decrease the number of strides for that session

94. The jumper should be able to execute his/her approach run blindfolded

95. Long jumping over a hurdle helps the ability to correctly penetrate the board during takeoff

96. Using cone targets during triple jump phase work can help the athlete extend their distance

97. Performing a 5-10 minute cool jog will not make an athlete slower

98. Do all you can to look after your feet and ankles

99. Never skip the cool down section of a work out. When one workout ends you are always preparing for the next one

100. Do not get discouraged if your 100m time is slow. Remember, a male could run only an 11.5 second 100m but still be able to run 10.5 m/s over a fly 5m. Likewise a female could only a 13 second 100m but still be able to run 9 m/s over a fly 5m.

101. Always remember the things you love about training for the horizontal jumps. This journey is tough and will have many ups and downs along the way. Have fun!

Printed in Great Britain
by Amazon